eugene h. peterson

PROMISES
PROMISES
PROMISES

the
MESSAGE™
read. think. pray. live.

TH1NK
www.th1nkbooks.com

CONTENTS

Let the Word of Christ—the Message—have the run of the house. Give it plenty of room in your lives. Instruct and direct one another using good common sense. And sing, sing your hearts out to God! Let every detail in your lives— words, actions, whatever—be done in the name of the Master, Jesus, thanking God the Father every step of the way. — COLOSSIANS 3:16–17

The Bible gives us God's perspective. We can turn to it and check out what God thinks about us, things that we do and all aspects of life. This promise book is a tool. It isn't meant to replace reading the Bible and it's not meant to be read alone. If you look up a topic, have your Bible handy so you can look at the verses that surround these passages. When you read the verses that surround these selections, you'll gain a better understanding of the full meaning of the passage.

Our hope is that you'll turn to this book for encouragement in your everyday life. All of us go through times when we struggle with certain areas of our life and don't know what to think, what to say, what to do, what to be. It's at those points that we need encouragement, hope and direction.

Taken from The Message, these passages are written in the kind of contemporary language we use every day. Please use this as a source of encouragement and direction.

Watch your step. Use your head. Make the most of every chance you get. These are desperate times! — **EPHESIANS** 5:15-16

Don't push your way to the front; don't sweet-talk your way to the top. Put yourself aside, and help others get ahead. — **PHILIPPIANS** 2:3

Stay calm; mind your own business; do your own job.
— **1 THESSALONIANS** 4:11

Mean-spirited ambition isn't wisdom. Boasting that you are wise isn't wisdom. Twisting the truth to make yourselves sound wise isn't wisdom.
— **JAMES** 3:14

And now I have a word for you who brashly announce, "Today — at the latest, tomorrow — we're off to such and such a city for the year. We're going to start a business and make a lot of money." You don't know the first thing about tomorrow. You're nothing but a wisp of fog, catching a brief bit of sun before disappearing. Instead, make it a habit to say, "If the Master wills it and we're still alive, we'll do this or that."

As it is, you are full of your grandiose selves. All such vaunting self-importance is evil. — **JAMES** 4:13-16

Slowness to anger makes for deep understanding;
    a quick-tempered person stockpiles stupidity. — PROVERBS 14:29

A gentle response defuses anger,
    but a sharp tongue kindles a temper-fire. — PROVERBS 15:1

Let angry people endure the backlash of their own anger;
    if you try to make it better, you'll only make it worse.
— PROVERBS 19:19

Don't hang out with angry people;
    don't keep company with hotheads.
Bad temper is contagious —
    don't get infected. — PROVERBS 22:24-25

A gang of cynics can upset a whole city;
    a group of sages can calm everyone down.

A sage trying to work things out with a fool
    gets only scorn and sarcasm for his trouble. — PROVERBS 29:8-9

[Jesus said,] "You're familiar with the command to the ancients, 'Do not murder.' I'm telling you that anyone who is so much as angry with a brother or sister is guilty of murder. . . . The simple moral fact is that words kill." — **MATTHEW** 5:21-22

Don't insist on getting even; that's not for you to do. "I'll do the judging," says God. "I'll take care of it." — **ROMANS** 12:19

When someone gets to the end of his rope, I feel the desperation in my bones. When someone is duped into sin, an angry fire burns in my gut. — 2 **CORINTHIANS** 11:29

Since prayer is at the bottom of all this, what I want mostly is for men to pray — not shaking angry fists at enemies but raising holy hands to God. — 1 **TIMOTHY** 2:8

ASSURANCE

You're well-known as good and forgiving,
bighearted to all who ask for help.
Pay attention, GOD, to my prayer;
bend down and listen to my cry for help.
Every time I'm in trouble I call on you,
confident that you'll answer. — **PSALM** 86:5-7

Your GOD is present among you,
a strong Warrior there to save you.
Happy to have you back, he'll calm you with his love
and delight you with his songs. — **ZEPHANIAH** 3:17

In alert expectancy such as this, we're never left feeling shortchanged. Quite the contrary — we can't round up enough containers to hold everything God generously pours into our lives through the Holy Spirit! — ROMANS 5:5

BELIEF

"Your eyes are windows into your body. If you open your eyes wide in wonder and belief, your body fills up with light." — MATTHEW 6:22

"This is how much God loved the world: He gave his Son, his one and only Son. And this is why: so that no one need be destroyed; by believing in him, anyone can have a whole and lasting life." — JOHN 3:16

[Jesus said,] "I am Light that has come into the world so that all who believe in me won't have to stay any longer in the dark."
— JOHN 12:46

Jesus said, "So, you believe because you've seen with your own eyes. Even better blessings are in store for those who believe without seeing."
— JOHN 20:29

Those who think they can do it on their own end up obsessed with measuring their own moral muscle but never get around to exercising it in real life. Those who trust God's action in them find that God's Spirit is in them — living and breathing God! — ROMANS 8:5

Before you trust, you have to listen. But unless Christ's Word is preached, there's nothing to listen to. — ROMANS 10:17

Keep your eyes open, hold tight to your convictions, give it all you've got, be resolute. — 1 CORINTHIANS 16:13

It's what we trust in but don't yet see that keeps us going.
— 2 CORINTHIANS 5:7

I have been crucified with Christ. My ego is no longer central. It is no longer important that I appear righteous before you or have your good opinion, and I am no longer driven to impress God. Christ lives in me. The life you see me living is not "mine," but it is lived by faith in the Son of God, who loved me and gave himself for me. — GALATIANS 2:20

Saving is all [God's] idea, and all his work. All we do is trust him enough to let him do it. It's God's gift from start to finish! We don't play the major role. If we did, we'd probably go around bragging that we'd done the whole thing! — EPHESIANS 2:8-9

We look at this Son and see the God who cannot be seen. We look at this Son and see God's original purpose in everything created. For everything, absolutely everything, above and below, visible and invisible, rank after rank after rank of angels — *everything* got started in him

and finds its purpose in him. He was there before any of it came into existence and holds it all together right up to this moment.
— **COLOSSIANS** 1:15-17

The fundamental fact of existence is that this trust in God, this faith, is the firm foundation under everything that makes life worth living. It's our handle on what we can't see. — **HEBREWS** 11:1

By faith, we see the world called into existence by God's word, what we see created by what we don't see. — **HEBREWS** 11:3

It's impossible to please God apart from faith. And why? Because anyone who wants to approach God must believe both that he exists *and* that he cares enough to respond to those who seek him.
— **HEBREWS** 11:6

You know that under pressure, your faith-life is forced into the open and shows its true colors. — **JAMES** 1:3

Do you think you'll get anywhere in this if you learn all the right words but never do anything? Does merely talking about faith indicate that a person really has it? For instance, you come upon an old friend dressed in rags and half-starved and say, "Good morning, friend! Be clothed in Christ! Be filled with the Holy Spirit!" and walk off without providing so much as a coat or a cup of soup — where does that

PROMISES. PROMISES. PROMISES.

get you? Isn't it obvious that God-talk without God-acts is outrageous nonsense? — JAMES 2:14-17

Pure gold put in the fire comes out of it *proved* pure; genuine faith put through this suffering comes out *proved* genuine. When Jesus wraps this all up, it's your faith, not your gold, that God will have on display as evidence of his victory. — 1 PETER 1:7

So don't lose a minute in building on what you've been given, complementing your basic faith with good character, spiritual understanding, alert discipline, passionate patience, reverent wonder, warm friendliness, and generous love, each dimension fitting into and developing the others. — 2 PETER 1:5-7

Anyone who gets so progressive in his thinking that he walks out on the teaching of Christ, walks out on God. — 2 JOHN 9

CHANGE

[Jesus said,] "I've come to change everything, turn everything rightside up." — LUKE 12:50

"You know how to tell a change in the weather, so don't tell me you can't tell a change in the season, the God-season we're in right now." — LUKE 12:56

"It's time to change your ways! Turn to face God so he can wipe away your sins, pour out showers of blessing to refresh you." — ACTS 3:19

Did you think that because he's such a nice God, he'd let you off the hook? Better think this one through from the beginning. God is kind, but he's not soft. In kindness he takes us firmly by the hand and leads us into a radical life-change. — ROMANS 2:4

If God himself has taken up residence in your life, you can hardly be thinking more of yourself than of him. Anyone, of course, who has not welcomed this invisible but clearly present God, the Spirit of Christ, won't know what we're talking about. But for you who welcome him, in whom he dwells — even though you still experience all the limitations of sin — you yourself experience life on God's terms. — ROMANS 8:9-10

Embracing what God does for you is the best thing you can do for him. Don't become so well-adjusted to your culture that you fit into it without even thinking. Instead, fix your attention on God. You'll be changed from the inside out. Readily recognize what he wants from you, and quickly respond to it. Unlike the culture around you, always dragging you down to its level of immaturity, God brings the best out of you, develops well-formed maturity in you. — ROMANS 12:1-2

Now we look inside, and what we see is that anyone united with the Messiah gets a fresh start, is created new. The old life is gone; a new life burgeons! — 2 CORINTHIANS 5:17

Earlier, before you knew God personally, you were enslaved to so-called gods that had nothing of the divine about them. But now that you know the real God — or rather since God knows you — how can you possibly subject yourselves again to those paper tigers?
— GALATIANS 4:8-9

God's readiness to give and forgive is now public. Salvation's available for everyone! We're being shown how to turn our backs on a godless, indulgent life, and how to take on a God-filled, God-honoring life. This new life is starting right now. — TITUS 2:11-12

Jesus doesn't change — yesterday, today, tomorrow, he's always totally himself. — HEBREWS 13:8

Now that you've cleaned up your lives by following the truth, love one another as if your lives depended on it. Your new life is not like your old life. Your old birth came from mortal sperm; your new birth comes from God's living Word. Just think: a life conceived by God himself!
— 1 PETER 1:22-23

God isn't late with his promise as some measure lateness. He is restraining himself on account of you, holding back the End because he doesn't want anyone lost. He's giving everyone space and time to change. — 2 PETER 3:9

CHILD of GOD

My father and mother walked out and left me,
    but GOD took me in. — **PSALM** 27:10

You got me when I was an unformed youth,
    God, and taught me everything I know.
Now I'm telling the world your wonders;
    I'll keep at it until I'm old and gray. — **PSALM** 71:17-18

How can a young person live a clean life?
    By carefully reading the map of your Word. — **PSALM** 119:9

Oh listen, dear child—become wise;
    point your life in the right direction. — **PROVERBS** 23:19

The disciples came to Jesus asking, "Who gets the highest rank in God's kingdom?"

For an answer Jesus called over a child, whom he stood in the middle of the room, and said, "I'm telling you, once and for all, that unless you return to square one and start over like children, you're not even going to get a look at the kingdom, let alone get in. Whoever becomes simple and elemental again, like this child, will rank high in God's kingdom. What's more, when you receive the childlike on my account, it's the same as receiving me." — **MATTHEW** 18:1-5

One day children were brought to Jesus in the hope that he would lay hands on them and pray over them. The disciples shooed them off. But Jesus intervened: "Let the children alone, don't prevent them from coming to me. God's kingdom is made up of people like these."
— MATTHEW 19:13-14

Watch what God does, and then you do it, like children who learn proper behavior from their parents. — EPHESIANS 5:1

As obedient children, let yourselves be pulled into a way of life shaped by God's life, a life energetic and blazing with holiness.
— 1 PETER 1:15

CHOICES

I say to GOD, "Be my Lord!"
   Without you, nothing makes sense. — PSALM 16:2

My choice is you, GOD, first and only.
   And now I find I'm *your* choice! — PSALM 16:5

We plan the way we want to live,
   but only GOD makes us able to live it. — PROVERBS 16:9

Get wisdom — it's worth more than money;
    choose insight over income every time. — **PROVERBS** 16:16

Words kill, words give life;
    they're either poison or fruit — you choose. — **PROVERBS** 18:21

Isn't it obvious that God deliberately chose men and women that the culture overlooks and exploits and abuses, chose these "nobodies" to expose the hollow pretensions of the "somebodies"?
— **1 CORINTHIANS** 1:27-28

If you choose to speak, you're also responsible for how and when you speak. — **1 CORINTHIANS** 14:32

There are many out there taking other paths, choosing other goals, and trying to get you to go along with them. — **PHILIPPIANS** 3:18

COMFORT

GOD's a safe-house for the battered,
    a sanctuary during bad times. — **PSALM** 9:9

God is a safe place to hide,
    ready to help when we need him. — **PSALM** 46:1

Pile your troubles on GOD's shoulders—
> he'll carry your load, he'll help you out. — **PSALM** 55:22

[God] heals the heartbroken
> and bandages their wounds. — **PSALM** 147:3

Our Lord is great, with limitless strength;
> we'll never comprehend what he knows and does.

GOD puts the fallen on their feet again. — **PSALM** 147:5-6

[Jesus said,] "Are you tired? Worn out? Burned out on religion? Come to me. Get away with me and you'll recover your life. I'll show you how to take a real rest." — **MATTHEW** 11:28

"I will talk to the Father, and he'll provide you another Friend so that you will always have someone with you. This Friend is the Spirit of Truth. The godless world can't take him in because it doesn't have eyes to see him, doesn't know what to look for. But you know him already because he has been staying with you, and will even be *in* you!

"I will not leave you orphaned. I'm coming back."
— **JOHN** 14:16-18

"I've told you all this so that trusting me, you will be unshakable and assured, deeply at peace. In this godless world you will continue to experience difficulties. But take heart! I've conquered the world."
— **JOHN** 16:33

We have plenty of hard times that come from following the Messiah, but no more so than the good times of his healing comfort — we get a full measure of that, too. — 2 CORINTHIANS 1:5

We're not giving up. How could we! Even though on the outside it often looks like things are falling apart on us, on the inside, where God is making new life, not a day goes by without his unfolding grace. . . . There's far more here than meets the eye. The things we see now are here today, gone tomorrow. But the things we can't see now will last forever. — 2 CORINTHIANS 4:16,18

May Jesus himself and God our Father, who reached out in love and surprised you with gifts of unending help and confidence, put a fresh heart in you, invigorate your work, enliven your speech.
— 2 THESSALONIANS 2:16-17

COMPROMISE

[Jesus said,] "Stand up for me against world opinion and I'll stand up for you before my Father in heaven. If you turn tail and run, do you think I'll cover for you?" — MATTHEW 10:32-33

Don't become so well-adjusted to your culture that you fit into it without even thinking. Instead, fix your attention on God. You'll be changed from the inside out. Readily recognize what he wants from you, and quickly respond to it. Unlike the culture around you, always dragging you down to its level of immaturity, God brings the best out of you, develops well-formed maturity in you. — ROMANS 12:2

Don't become partners with those who reject God. How can you make a partnership out of right and wrong? That's not partnership; that's war. Is light best friends with dark? . . .
"So leave the corruption and compromise;
leave it for good," says God.
"Don't link up with those who will pollute you.
I want you all for myself." — 2 CORINTHIANS 6:14,17

Don't let yourselves get taken in by religious smooth talk. God gets furious with people who are full of religious sales talk but want nothing to do with him. — EPHESIANS 5:6

God tested us thoroughly to make sure we were qualified to be trusted with this Message. Be assured that when we speak to you we're not after crowd approval—only God approval. Since we've been put through that battery of tests, you're guaranteed that both we and the Message are free of error, mixed motives, or hidden agendas.
— 1 THESSALONIANS 2:3-4

Anyone who gets so progressive in his thinking that he walks out on the teaching of Christ, walks out on God. — 2 JOHN 9

[Jesus said,] "I know you inside and out, and find little to my liking. You're not cold, you're not hot — far better to be either cold or hot! You're stale. You're stagnant." — REVELATION 3:15-16

CONFIDENCE

With [God] on my side I'm fearless,
   afraid of no one and nothing. — PSALM 27:1

There's no such thing as self-rescue,
   pulling yourself up by your bootstraps. — PSALM 49:7

Every time I'm in trouble I call on you, [God,]
   confident that you'll answer. — PSALM 86:7

Far better to take refuge in GOD
   than trust in people. — PSALM 118:8

The wicked are edgy with guilt, ready to run off
   even when no one's after them;
Honest people are relaxed and confident,
   bold as lions. — PROVERBS 28:1

Don't be so naive and self-confident. You're not exempt. You could fall flat on your face as easily as anyone else. Forget about self-confidence; it's useless. Cultivate God-confidence. — 1 CORINTHIANS 10:12

Stand your ground. And don't hold back. Throw yourselves into the work of the Master, confident that nothing you do for him is a waste of time or effort. — 1 CORINTHIANS 15:58

There's far more here than meets the eye. The things we see now are here today, gone tomorrow. But the things we can't see now will last forever. — 2 CORINTHIANS 4:18

There has never been the slightest doubt in my mind that the God who started this great work in you would keep at it and bring it to a flourishing finish on the very day Christ Jesus appears.
— PHILIPPIANS 1:6

Whatever I have, wherever I am, I can make it through anything in the One who makes me who I am. — PHILIPPIANS 4:13

I want you woven into a tapestry of love, in touch with everything there is to know of God. Then you will have minds confident and at rest, focused on Christ, God's great mystery. — COLOSSIANS 2:2

God doesn't want us to be shy with his gifts, but bold and loving and sensible. — 2 TIMOTHY 1:7

CONSCIENCE

I know how bad I've been;
>   my sins are staring me down. — **PSALM** 51:3

"Your eye is a lamp, lighting up your whole body. If you live wide-eyed in wonder and belief, your body fills up with light. If you live squinty-eyed in greed and distrust, your body is a dank cellar." — **LUKE** 11:34

"I do my level best to keep a clear conscience before God and my neighbors in everything I do." — **ACTS** 24:16

When outsiders who have never heard of God's law follow it more or less by instinct, they confirm its truth by their obedience. They show that God's law is not something alien, imposed on us from without, but woven into the very fabric of our creation. There is something deep within them that echoes God's yes and no, right and wrong.
— **ROMANS** 2:14-15

If you notice that you are acting in ways inconsistent with what you believe — some days trying to impose your opinions on others, other days just trying to please them — then you know that you're out of line. If the way you live isn't consistent with what you believe, then it's wrong. — **ROMANS** 14:23

Now that the worst is over, we're pleased we can report that we've come out of this with conscience and faith intact, and can face the world. . . . But it wasn't by any fancy footwork on our part. It was God who kept us focused on him, uncompromised.

— 2 CORINTHIANS 1:12

If you know the right thing to do and don't do it, that, for you, is evil.

— JAMES 4:17

Keep a clear conscience before God so that when people throw mud at you, none of it will stick. They'll end up realizing that they're the ones who need a bath. — 1 PETER 3:16

Let's not just talk about love; let's practice real love. This is the only way we'll know we're living truly, living in God's reality. It's also the way to shut down debilitating self-criticism, even when there is something to it. For God is greater than our worried hearts and knows more about us than we do ourselves. — 1 JOHN 3:18-20

CONTENTMENT

I'd rather scrub floors in the house of my God
    than be honored as a guest in the palace of sin.

— PSALM 84:10

A pretentious, showy life is an empty life;
   a plain and simple life is a full life. — **PROVERBS** 13:7

"If you walk around with your nose in the air, you're going to end up flat on your face. But if you're content to be simply yourself, you will become more than yourself." — **LUKE** 14:11

As long as you grab for what makes you feel good or makes you look important, are you really much different than a babe at the breast, content only when everything's going your way? — 1 **CORINTHIANS** 3:3

Actually, I don't have a sense of needing anything personally. I've learned by now to be quite content whatever my circumstances. I'm just as happy with little as with much, with much as with little. I've found the recipe for being happy whether full or hungry, hands full or hands empty. Whatever I have, wherever I am, I can make it through anything in the One who makes me who I am.
— **PHILIPPIANS** 4:11-13

Be content with obscurity, like Christ. — **COLOSSIANS** 3:4

We loved you dearly. Not content to just pass on the Message, we wanted to give you our hearts. And we *did*. — 1 **THESSALONIANS** 2:8

A devout life does bring wealth, but it's the rich simplicity of being yourself before God. Since we entered the world penniless and will leave it penniless, if we have bread on the table and shoes on our feet, that's enough. — 1 TIMOTHY 6:6-8

Don't be obsessed with getting more material things. Be relaxed with what you have. Since God assured us, "I'll never let you down, never walk off and leave you." — HEBREWS 13:5

So be content with who you are, and don't put on airs. God's strong hand is on you; he'll promote you at the right time. Live carefree before God; he is most careful with you. — 1 PETER 5:6-7

CRITICISM

[Jesus said,] "Count yourself blessed every time someone cuts you down or throws you out, every time someone smears or blackens your name to discredit me. What it means is that the truth is too close for comfort and that that person is uncomfortable." — LUKE 6:22

"Don't pick on people, jump on their failures, criticize their faults — unless, of course, you want the same treatment. Don't condemn those who are down; that hardness can boomerang. Be easy on people; you'll find life a lot easier." — LUKE 6:37

Every time you criticize someone, you condemn yourself. It takes one to know one. Judgmental criticism of others is a well-known way of escaping detection in your own crimes and misdemeanors.
— ROMANS 2:1

It matters very little to me what you think of me, even less where I rank in popular opinion. I don't even rank myself. Comparisons in these matters are pointless. I'm not aware of anything that would disqualify me from being a good guide for you, but that doesn't mean much. The *Master* makes that judgment.

So don't get ahead of the Master and jump to conclusions with your judgments before all the evidence is in. When he comes, he will bring out in the open and place in evidence all kinds of things we never even dreamed of—inner motives and purposes and prayers. Only then will any one of us get to hear the "Well done!" of God.
— 1 CORINTHIANS 4:3-5

God's people should be bighearted and courteous. It wasn't so long ago that we ourselves were stupid and stubborn, dupes of sin, ordered every which way by our glands, going around with a chip on our shoulder, hated and hating back. — TITUS 3:2-3

Don't bad-mouth each other, friends. It's God's Word, his Message, his Royal Rule, that takes a beating in that kind of talk. You're supposed to be honoring the Message, not writing graffiti all over it. — JAMES 4:11

Jesus [said,] "First things first. Your business is life, not death. Follow me. Pursue life." — MATTHEW 8:22

When it's sin versus grace, grace wins hands down. All sin can do is threaten us with death, and that's the end of it. Grace, because God is putting everything together again through the Messiah, invites us into life — a life that goes on and on and on, world without end.
— ROMANS 5:20-21

What we believe is this: If we get included in Christ's sin-conquering death, we also get included in his life-saving resurrection. We know that when Jesus was raised from the dead it was a signal of the end of death-as-the-end. Never again will death have the last word.
— ROMANS 6:8-9

Work hard for sin your whole life and your pension is death. But God's gift is real life, eternal life, delivered by Jesus, our Master.
— ROMANS 6:23

I look death in the face practically every day I live. Do you think I'd do this if I wasn't convinced of your resurrection and mine as guaranteed by the resurrected Messiah Jesus? — 1 CORINTHIANS 15:31

Your old life is dead. Your new life, which is your *real* life — even though invisible to spectators — is with Christ in God. *He* is your life.
— COLOSSIANS 3:3

DEPRESSION

I waited and waited and waited for GOD.
　　At last he looked; finally he listened.
He lifted me out of the ditch,
　　pulled me from deep mud.
He stood me up on a solid rock
　　to make sure I wouldn't slip.
He taught me how to sing the latest God-song,
　　a praise-song to our God.
More and more people are seeing this:
　　they enter the mystery,
　　abandoning themselves to GOD. — PSALM 40:1-3

GOD is a safe place to hide,
　　ready to help when we need him.
We stand fearless at the cliff-edge of doom. — PSALM 46:1-2

Pile your troubles on GOD's shoulders —
　　he'll carry your load, he'll help you out. — PSALM 55:22

The person who shuns the bitter moments of friends
　　will be an outsider at their celebrations. — PROVERBS 14:10

A cheerful disposition is good for your health;
    gloom and doom leave you bone-tired. — **PROVERBS** 17:22

[Jesus said,] "Are you tired? Worn out? Burned out on religion? Come to me. Get away with me and you'll recover your life. I'll show you how to take a real rest. Walk with me and work with me — watch how I do it. Learn the unforced rhythms of grace. I won't lay anything heavy or ill-fitting on you. Keep company with me and you'll learn to live freely and lightly." — **MATTHEW** 11:28-30

Yes. I'm full of myself — after all, I've spent a long time in sin's prison. What I don't understand about myself is that I decide one way, but then I act another, doing things I absolutely despise. . . .

I realize that I don't have what it takes. I can will it, but I can't *do* it. I decide to do good, but I don't *really* do it; I decide not to do bad, but then I do it anyway. My decisions, such as they are, don't result in actions. Something has gone wrong deep within me and gets the better of me every time.

It happens so regularly that it's predictable. The moment I decide to do good, sin is there to trip me up. I truly delight in God's commands, but it's pretty obvious that not all of me joins in that delight. Parts of me covertly rebel, and just when I least expect it, they take charge.

I've tried everything and nothing helps. I'm at the end of my rope. Is there no one who can do anything for me? Isn't that the real question?

The answer, thank God, is that Jesus Christ can and does. He acted to set things right in this life of contradictions where I want to serve God with all my heart and mind, but am pulled by the influence of sin to do something totally different. — **ROMANS** 7:14-15,18-25

All praise to the God and Father of our Master, Jesus the Messiah! Father of all mercy! God of all healing counsel! He comes alongside us when we go through hard times, and before you know it, he brings us alongside someone else who is going through hard times so that we can be there for that person just as God was there for us. . . .

It was so bad we didn't think we were going to make it. We felt like we'd been sent to death row, that it was all over for us. As it turned out, it was the best thing that could have happened. Instead of trusting in our own strength or wits to get out of it, we were forced to trust God totally — not a bad idea since he's the God who raises the dead! And he did it, rescued us from certain doom. *And* he'll do it again, rescuing us as many times as we need rescuing. You and your prayers are part of the rescue operation. — 2 CORINTHIANS 1:3-4,8-11

We've been surrounded and battered by troubles, but we're not demoralized; we're not sure what to do, but we know that God knows what to do; we've been spiritually terrorized, but God hasn't left our side; we've been thrown down, but we haven't broken.
— 2 CORINTHIANS 4:8-9

Now we look inside, and what we see is that anyone united with the Messiah gets a fresh start, is created new. The old life is gone; a new life burgeons! Look at it! — 2 CORINTHIANS 5:17

When life gets really difficult, don't jump to the conclusion that God isn't on the job. Instead, be glad that you are in the very thick of what

Christ experienced. This is a spiritual refining process, with glory just around the corner. — 1 PETER 4:12-13

DIRECTION

Clean the slate, God, so we can start the day fresh!
> Keep me from stupid sins,
> from thinking I can take over your work. — PSALM 19:13

GOD is fair and just;
He corrects the misdirected,
Sends them in the right direction. — PSALM 25:8

Bring me back from gray exile,
> put a fresh wind in my sails! — PSALM 51:12

[God,] I'm your servant — help me understand what that means,
> the inner meaning of your instructions.
Break open your words, let the light shine out,
> let ordinary people see the meaning. — PSALM 119:125,130

Trust GOD from the bottom of your heart;
> don't try to figure out everything on your own.
Listen for GOD's voice in everything you do, everywhere you go;
> he's the one who will keep you on track.

Don't assume that you know it all.
Run to GOD! Run from evil! — PROVERBS 3:5-7

Without good direction, people lose their way;
the more wise counsel you follow, the better your chances.
— PROVERBS 11:14

There's a way that looks harmless enough;
look again — it leads straight to hell. — PROVERBS 16:25

People ruin their lives by their own stupidity,
so why does GOD always get blamed? — PROVERBS 19:3

[Jesus said,] "Anyone who intends to come with me has to let me lead.
You're not in the driver's seat — I am." — LUKE 9:23

[Jesus said,] "I am the world's Light. No one who follows me stumbles
around in the darkness. I provide plenty of light to live in."
— JOHN 8:12

Jesus said, "I am the Road, also the Truth, also the Life. No one gets
to the Father apart from me." — JOHN 14:6

What happened was this: People knew God perfectly well, but when they didn't treat him like God, refusing to worship him, they trivialized themselves into silliness and confusion so that there was neither sense nor direction left in their lives. — **ROMANS** 1:21

I have a special word of caution for you who are sure that you have it all together yourselves and, because you know God's revealed Word inside and out, feel qualified to guide others through their blind alleys and dark nights and confused emotions to God. — **ROMANS** 2:19-20

Who in the world do you think you are to second-guess God? Do you for one moment suppose any of us knows enough to call God into question? — **ROMANS** 9:20

Figure out what will please Christ, and then do it. — **EPHESIANS** 5:10

Let the peace of Christ keep you in tune with each other, in step with each other. None of this going off and doing your own thing.
— **COLOSSIANS** 3:15

It's true that moral guidance and counsel need to be given, but the way you say it and to whom you say it are as important as what you say.
— **1 TIMOTHY** 1:8

You need to stick it out, staying with God's plan so you'll be there for the promised completion.
— **HEBREWS** 10:36

If you find life difficult because you're doing what God said, take it in stride. Trust him. He knows what he's doing, and he'll keep on doing it. — **1 PETER** 4:19

DISCIPLINE

Don't, dear friend, resent GOD's discipline;
    don't sulk under his loving correction.
It's the child he loves that GOD corrects. — **PROVERBS** 3:11-12

If you love learning, you love the discipline that goes with it —
    how shortsighted to refuse correction! — **PROVERBS** 12:1

A good thrashing purges evil;
    punishment goes deep within us. — **PROVERBS** 20:30

For people who hate discipline
    and only get more stubborn,
There'll come a day when life tumbles in and they break,
    but by then it'll be too late to help them. — **PROVERBS** 29:1

"You're blessed when your commitment to God provokes persecution. The persecution drives you even deeper into God's kingdom."
— **MATTHEW** 5:10

Examine your motives, test your heart. — 1 **CORINTHIANS** 11:28

Live creatively, friends. If someone falls into sin, forgivingly restore him, saving your critical comments for yourself. You might be needing forgiveness before the day's out. — **GALATIANS** 6:1

God is educating you; that's why you must never drop out. He's treating you as dear children. This trouble you're in isn't punishment; it's *training*, the normal experience of children. Only irresponsible parents leave children to fend for themselves. Would you prefer an irresponsible God? We respect our own parents for training and not spoiling us, so why not embrace God's training so we can truly *live*? While we were children, our parents did what *seemed* best to them. But God is doing what *is* best for us, training us to live God's holy best. At the time, discipline isn't much fun. It always feels like it's going against the grain. Later, of course, it pays off handsomely, for it's the well-trained who find themselves mature in their relationship with God.
— **HEBREWS** 12:7-11

What counts is that you put up with it for God's sake when you're treated badly for no good reason. There's no particular virtue in accepting punishment that you well deserve. But if you're treated badly for good behavior and continue in spite of it to be a good servant, that is what counts with God. — 1 PETER 2:19-20

DOUBT

[Abraham] didn't tiptoe around God's promise asking cautiously skeptical questions. He plunged into the promise and came up strong, ready for God. — ROMANS 4:20

You let the world, which doesn't know the first thing about living, tell you how to live. You filled your lungs with polluted unbelief, and then exhaled disobedience. We all did it, all of us doing what we felt like doing, when we felt like doing it, all of us in the same boat. It's a wonder God didn't lose his temper and do away with the whole lot of us. — EPHESIANS 2:2-3

Make sure there's no evil unbelief lying around that will trip you up and throw you off course, diverting you from the living God. — HEBREWS 3:12

God means what he says. What he says goes. His powerful Word is sharp as a surgeon's scalpel, cutting through everything, whether doubt or defense, laying us open to listen and obey. — HEBREWS 4:12

My purpose is simply this: that you who believe in God's Son will know beyond the shadow of a doubt that you have eternal life, the reality and not the illusion.
— 1 JOHN 5:13

Go easy on those who hesitate in the faith. Go after those who take the wrong way. Be tender with sinners, but not soft on sin. The sin itself stinks to high heaven. — JUDE 22-23

ENCOURAGEMENT

Stay with GOD!
    Take heart. Don't quit.
I'll say it again:
    Stay with GOD. — PSALM 27:14

Be brave. Be strong. Don't give up.
    Expect GOD to get here soon. — PSALM 31:24

Never walk away from someone who deserves help;
    your hand is God's hand for that person. — PROVERBS 3:27

Gracious speech is like clover honey —
    good taste to the soul, quick energy for the body.
— PROVERBS 16:24

If you give encouraging guidance, be careful that you don't get bossy; if you're put in charge, don't manipulate; if you're called to give aid to people in distress, keep your eyes open and be quick to respond; if you work with the disadvantaged, don't let yourself get irritated with them or depressed by them. Keep a smile on your face. — ROMANS 12:8

Those of us who are strong and able in the faith need to step in and lend a hand to those who falter, and not just do what is most convenient for us. Strength is for service, not status. — ROMANS 15:1

[God] comes alongside us when we go through hard times, and before you know it, he brings us alongside someone else who is going through hard times so that we can be there for that person just as God was there for us. — 2 CORINTHIANS 1:4

We've been surrounded and battered by troubles, but we're not demoralized; we're not sure what to do, but we know that God knows what to do; we've been spiritually terrorized, but God hasn't left our side; we've been thrown down, but we haven't broken.
— 2 CORINTHIANS 4:8-9

Even though on the outside it often looks like things are falling apart on us, on the inside, where God is making new life, not a day goes by without his unfolding grace. — 2 CORINTHIANS 4:16

Gently encourage the stragglers, and reach out for the exhausted, pulling them to their feet. Be patient with each person, attentive to individual needs. — 1 THESSALONIANS 5:14

Let's see how inventive we can be in encouraging love and helping out. — HEBREWS 10:24

EXCELLENCE

"In a word, what I'm saying is, *Grow up*. You're kingdom subjects. Now live like it. Live out your God-created identity. Live generously and graciously toward others, the way God lives toward you." — MATTHEW 5:48

I'm running hard for the finish line. I'm giving it everything I've got. No sloppy living for me! — 1 CORINTHIANS 9:26

You do so well in so many things — you trust God, you're articulate, you're insightful, you're passionate, you love us — now, do your best in this, too. — 2 CORINTHIANS 8:7

You'll do best by filling your minds and meditating on things true, noble, reputable, authentic, compelling, gracious — the best, not the worst; the beautiful, not the ugly; things to praise, not things to curse. Put into practice what you learned from me, what you heard and saw

and realized. Do that, and God, who makes everything work together, will work you into his most excellent harmonies.
— PHILIPPIANS 4:8-9

FAMILY

How wonderful, how beautiful,
        when brothers and sisters get along! — PSALM 133:1

Exploit or abuse your family, and end up with a fistful of air.
— PROVERBS 11:29

A greedy and grasping person destroys community.
— PROVERBS 15:27

Old people are distinguished by grandchildren;
        children take pride in their parents. — PROVERBS 17:6

It takes wisdom to build a house,
        and understanding to set it on a firm foundation.
— PROVERBS 24:3

"You're blessed when you can show people how to cooperate instead of compete or fight. That's when you discover who you really are, and your place in God's family." — MATTHEW 5:9

[Jesus said,] "Obedience is thicker than blood. The person who obeys God's will is my brother and sister and mother." — MARK 3:35

Wives, understand and support your husbands by submitting to them in ways that honor the Master.

Husbands, go all out in love for your wives. Don't take advantage of them.

Children, do what your parents tell you. This delights the Master no end.

Parents, don't come down too hard on your children or you'll crush their spirits. — COLOSSIANS 3:18-21

Take care of widows who are destitute. If a widow has family members to take care of her, let them learn that religion begins at their own doorstep and that they should pay back with gratitude some of what they have received. This pleases God immensely. . . .

Anyone who neglects to care for family members in need repudiates the faith. That's worse than refusing to believe in the first place.
— 1 TIMOTHY 5:3-4,8

FEAR

With [God] on my side I'm fearless,
    afraid of no one and nothing. — PSALM 27:1

"Don't be bluffed into silence by the threats of bullies. There's nothing they can do to your soul, your core being. Save your fear for God, who holds your entire life — body and soul — in his hands." — MATTHEW 10:28

Jesus reprimanded the disciples: "Why are you such cowards? Don't you have any faith at all?" — MARK 4:40

God is there, ready to help;
I'm fearless no matter what.
Who or what can get to me? — HEBREWS 13:6

There is no room in love for fear. Well-formed love banishes fear. Since fear is crippling, a fearful life — fear of death, fear of judgment — is one not yet fully formed in love. — 1 JOHN 4:18

FORGIVENESS

As far as sunrise is from sunset,
    [God] has separated us from our sins. — PSALM 103:12

Smart people know how to hold their tongue;
    their grandeur is to forgive and forget. — PROVERBS 19:11

"In prayer there is a connection between what God does and what you do. You can't get forgiveness from God, for instance, without also forgiving others. If you refuse to do your part, you cut yourself off from God's part." — MATTHEW 6:14-15

Peter got up the nerve to ask, "Master, how many times do I forgive a brother or sister who hurts me? Seven?"

Jesus replied, "Seven! Hardly. Try seventy times seven."
— **MATTHEW** 18:21-22

"Listen to this carefully. I'm warning you. There's nothing done or said that can't be forgiven. But if you persist in your slanders against God's Holy Spirit, you are repudiating the very One who forgives, sawing off the branch on which you're sitting, severing by your own perversity all connection with the One who forgives." — **MARK** 3:28-29

"When you assume the posture of prayer, remember that it's not all *asking*. If you have anything against someone, *forgive* — only then will your heavenly Father be inclined to also wipe your slate clean of sins."
— **MARK** 11:25

"Impressive, isn't it? She was forgiven many, many sins, and so she is very, very grateful. If the forgiveness is minimal, the gratitude is minimal."
— **LUKE** 7:47

"If you forgive someone's sins, they're gone for good. If you don't forgive sins, what are you going to do with them?" — **JOHN** 20:23

All that passing laws against sin did was produce more lawbreakers. But sin didn't, and doesn't, have a chance in competition with the aggressive forgiveness we call *grace*. When it's sin versus grace, grace wins hands down. — **ROMANS** 5:20

Live creatively, friends. If someone falls into sin, forgivingly restore him, saving your critical comments for yourself. *You* might be needing forgiveness before the day's out. — **GALATIANS** 6:1

Be gentle with one another, sensitive. Forgive one another as quickly and thoroughly as God in Christ forgave you. — **EPHESIANS** 4:32

God's readiness to give and forgive is now public. Salvation's available for everyone! — **TITUS** 2:11

Make this your common practice: Confess your sins to each other and pray for each other so that you can live together whole and healed. The prayer of a person living right with God is something powerful to be reckoned with. — **JAMES** 5:16

Your sins are forgiven in Jesus' name. — 1 **JOHN** 2:12

FREEDOM

"Look at the birds, free and unfettered, not tied down to a job description, careless in the care of God. And you count far more to him than birds." — **MATTHEW** 6:26

[Jesus said,] "If you stick with this, living out what I tell you, you are my disciples for sure. Then you will experience for yourselves the truth, and the truth will free you." — JOHN 8:31-32

"If the Son sets you free, you are free through and through."
— JOHN 8:36

Sin can't tell you how to live. After all, you're not living under that old tyranny any longer. You're living in the freedom of God.

So, since we're out from under the old tyranny, does that mean we can live any old way we want? Since we're free in the freedom of God, can we do anything that comes to mind? Hardly. You know well enough from your own experience that there are some acts of so-called freedom that destroy freedom. Offer yourselves to sin, for instance, and it's your last free act. But offer yourselves to the ways of God and the freedom never quits. — ROMANS 6:14-16

Obsession with self in these matters is a dead end; attention to God leads us out into the open, into a spacious, free life. — ROMANS 8:6

Even though I am free of the demands and expectations of everyone, I have voluntarily become a servant to any and all in order to reach a wide range of people. — 1 CORINTHIANS 9:19

Don't be callous in your exercise of freedom, thoughtlessly stepping on the toes of those who aren't as free as you are.
— 1 CORINTHIANS 10:32

Is it not clear to you that to go back to that old rule-keeping, peer-pleasing religion would be an abandonment of everything personal and free in my relationship with God? I refuse to do that, to repudiate God's grace. If a living relationship with God could come by rule-keeping, then Christ died unnecessarily. — GALATIANS 2:21

Christ has set us free to live a free life. So take your stand! Never again let anyone put a harness of slavery on you. — GALATIANS 5:1

It is absolutely clear that God has called you to a free life. Just make sure that you don't use this freedom as an excuse to do whatever you want to do and destroy your freedom. Rather, use your freedom to serve one another in love; that's how freedom grows. For everything we know about God's Word is summed up in a single sentence: Love others as you love yourself. That's an act of true freedom. If you bite and ravage each other, watch out — in no time at all you will be annihilating each other, and where will your precious freedom be then?
— GALATIANS 5:13-15

Can't you see the central issue in all this? It is not what you and I do. . . . It is what *God* is doing, and he is creating something totally new, a free life! — GALATIANS 6:15

Whoever catches a glimpse of the revealed counsel of God — the free life! — even out of the corner of his eye, and sticks with it, is no distracted scatterbrain but a man or woman of action. That person will find delight and affirmation in the action. — JAMES 1:25

Then you'll be able to live out your days free to pursue what God wants instead of being tyrannized by what you want. — 1 PETER 4:2

Live carefree before God; he is most careful with you. — 1 PETER 5:7

FRIENDSHIP

God-friendship is for God-worshipers;
They are the ones he confides in. — PSALM 25:14

The person who shuns the bitter moments of friends
    will be an outsider at their celebrations. — PROVERBS 14:10

Do a favor and win a friend forever;
    nothing can untie that bond. — PROVERBS 18:19

Friends come and friends go,
    but a true friend sticks by you like family. — PROVERBS 18:24

Wealth attracts friends as honey draws flies,
but poor people are avoided like a plague. — PROVERBS 19:4

When you find a friend, don't outwear your welcome;
show up at all hours and he'll soon get fed up.
— PROVERBS 25:17

Just as lotions and fragrance give sensual delight,
a sweet friendship refreshes the soul. — PROVERBS 27:9

Don't leave your friends or your parents' friends
and run home to your family when things get rough;
Better a nearby friend
than a distant family. — PROVERBS 27:10

You use steel to sharpen steel,
and one friend sharpens another. — PROVERBS 27:17

"If a fellow believer hurts you, go and tell him — work it out between
the two of you. If he listens, you've made a friend." — MATTHEW 18:15

Laugh with your happy friends when they're happy; share tears when
they're down. Get along with each other; don't be stuck-up. Make friends
with nobodies; don't be the great somebody. — ROMANS 12:15-16

Become friends with God; he's already a friend with you.
— 2 CORINTHIANS 5:20

Agree with each other, love each other, be deep-spirited friends.
— PHILIPPIANS 2:2

GOSSIP

Don't talk out of both sides of your mouth;
   avoid careless banter, white lies, and gossip. — PROVERBS 4:24

A gadabout gossip can't be trusted with a secret,
   but someone of integrity won't violate a confidence.
— PROVERBS 11:13

Troublemakers start fights;
   gossips break up friendships. — PROVERBS 16:28

Listening to gossip is like eating cheap candy;
   do you really want junk like that in your belly?
— PROVERBS 18:8

When a leader listens to malicious gossip,
   all the workers get infected with evil. — PROVERBS 29:12

Watch the way you talk. Let nothing foul or dirty come out of your mouth. Say only what helps, each word a gift. — EPHESIANS 4:29

Though some tongues just love the taste of gossip, Christians have better uses for language than that. Don't talk dirty or silly. That kind of talk doesn't fit our style. Thanksgiving is our dialect. — EPHESIANS 5:4

Keep a clear conscience before God so that when people throw mud at you, none of it will stick. They'll end up realizing that they're the ones who need a bath. — 1 PETER 3:16

GREED

Why is everyone hungry for *more*? "More, more," they say.
"More, more."
I have God's more-than-enough. — PSALM 4:6

The world of the generous gets larger and larger;
    the world of the stingy gets smaller and smaller.
— PROVERBS 11:24

A greedy and grasping person destroys community. — PROVERBS 15:27

"Don't hoard treasure down here where it gets eaten by moths and corroded by rust or — worse! — stolen by burglars. Stockpile treasure in heaven, where it's safe from moth and rust and burglars. It's obvious, isn't it? The place where your treasure is, is the place you will most want to be, and end up being." — MATTHEW 6:19-21

"Give away your life; you'll find life given back, but not merely given back — given back with bonus and blessing. Giving, not getting, is the way. Generosity begets generosity." — LUKE 6:38

"Your eye is a lamp, lighting up your whole body. If you live wide-eyed in wonder and belief, your body fills up with light. If you live squinty-eyed in greed and distrust, your body is a dank cellar." — LUKE 11:34

"Take care! Protect yourself against the least bit of greed. Life is not defined by what you have, even when you have a lot." — LUKE 12:15

Your greedy luxuries are a cancer in your gut, destroying your life from within. You thought you were piling up wealth. What you've piled up is judgment. — JAMES 5:3

GRIEF

A hostile world! I call to GOD,
    I cry to God to help me.
From his palace he hears my call;
    my cry brings me right into his presence —
    a private audience! — PSALM 18:6

They hit me when I was down,
　　but GOD stuck by me. . . .
GOD made my life complete
　　when I placed all the pieces before him. — PSALM 18:18,20

God's eye is on those who respect him,
　　the ones who are looking for his love.
He's ready to come to their rescue in bad times;
　　in lean times he keeps body and soul together.
—PSALM 33:18-19

Is anyone crying for help? GOD is listening,
ready to rescue you.

If your heart is broken, you'll find GOD right there;
if you're kicked in the gut, he'll help you catch your breath.
— PSALM 34:17-18

Pile your troubles on GOD's shoulders —
　　he'll carry your load, he'll help you out. — PSALM 55:22

[God] heals the heartbroken
　　and bandages their wounds. — PSALM 147:3

Singing light songs to the heavyhearted
　　is like pouring salt in their wounds. — PROVERBS 25:20

"You're blessed when you feel you've lost what is most dear to you. Only then can you be embraced by the One most dear to you."
— MATTHEW 5:4

[Jesus said,] "I've told you all this so that trusting me, you will be unshakable and assured, deeply at peace. In this godless world you will continue to experience difficulties. But take heart! I've conquered the world." — JOHN 16:33

All praise to the God and Father of our Master, Jesus the Messiah! Father of all mercy! God of all healing counsel! He comes alongside us when we go through hard times, and before you know it, he brings us alongside someone else who is going through hard times so that we can be there for that person just as God was there for us. We have plenty of hard times that come from following the Messiah, but no more so than the good times of his healing comfort — we get a full measure of that, too.

When we suffer for Jesus, it works out for your healing and salvation. If we are treated well, given a helping hand and encouraging word, that also works to your benefit, spurring you on, face forward, unflinching. Your hard times are also our hard times. When we see that you're just as willing to endure the hard times as to enjoy the good times, we know you're going to make it, no doubt about it.
— 2 CORINTHIANS 1:3-7

It's what we trust in but don't yet see that keeps us going.
— 2 CORINTHIANS 5:7

Distress that drives us to God does that. It turns us around. It gets us back in the way of salvation. We never regret that kind of pain. But those who let distress drive them away from God are full of regrets, end up on a deathbed of regrets. — 2 CORINTHIANS 7:10

Don't grieve God. Don't break his heart. His Holy Spirit, moving and breathing in you, is the most intimate part of your life, making you fit for himself. Don't take such a gift for granted. — EPHESIANS 4:30

GUILT

Clean the slate, God, so we can start the day fresh!
    Keep me from stupid sins,
    from thinking I can take over your work;
Then I can start this day sun-washed,
    scrubbed clean of the grime of sin. — PSALM 19:13

Guilt is banished through love and truth. — PROVERBS 16:6

It's not right to go easy on the guilty,
    or come down hard on the innocent. — PROVERBS 18:5

The wicked are edgy with guilt, ready to run off
    even when no one's after them.
Honest people are relaxed and confident,
    bold as lions. — PROVERBS 28:1

You can't whitewash your sins and get by with it;
  you find mercy by admitting and leaving them.
— **PROVERBS** 28:13

"If you enter your place of worship and, about to make an offering, you suddenly remember a grudge a friend has against you, abandon your offering, leave immediately, go to this friend and make things right. Then and only then, come back and work things out with God."
— **MATTHEW** 5:23-24

"Everyone who makes a practice of doing evil, addicted to denial and illusion, hates God-light and won't come near it, fearing a painful exposure." — **JOHN** 3:20

"If you were really blind, you would be blameless, but since you claim to see everything so well, you're accountable for every fault and failure."
— **JOHN** 9:41

Every time you criticize someone, you condemn yourself. It takes one to know one. Judgmental criticism of others is a well-known way of escaping detection in your own crimes and misdemeanors. But God isn't so easily diverted. He sees right through all such smoke screens and holds you to what *you've* done.

You didn't think, did you, that just by pointing your finger at others you would distract God from seeing all your misdoings and from coming down on you hard? Or did you think that because he's such a

nice God, he'd let you off the hook? Better think this one through from the beginning. God is kind, but he's not soft. In kindness he takes us firmly by the hand and leads us into a radical life-change.
— **ROMANS** 2:1-4

Make this your common practice: Confess your sins to each other and pray for each other so that you can live together whole and healed. The prayer of a person living right with God is something powerful to be reckoned with. — **JAMES** 5:16

If we claim that we're free of sin, we're only fooling ourselves. A claim like that is errant nonsense. On the other hand, if we admit our sins — make a clean breast of them — he won't let us down; he'll be true to himself. He'll forgive our sins and purge us of all wrongdoing.
— 1 **JOHN** 1:8-9

HABITS

Now I'm alert to GOD's ways.
    I don't take God for granted. — **PSALM** 18:21

Make praise your habit. — **PSALM** 64:10

Form the habit of justice. — **PSALM** 106:3

Slack habits and sloppy work
are as bad as vandalism. — **PROVERBS** 18:9

All your lives you've let sin tell you what to do. But thank God you've started listening to a new master, one whose commands set you free to live openly in *his* freedom! — **ROMANS** 6:16-18

It is obvious what kind of life develops out of trying to get your own way all the time: repetitive, loveless, cheap sex; a stinking accumulation of mental and emotional garbage; frenzied and joyless grabs for happiness; trinket gods; magic-show religion; paranoid loneliness; cutthroat competition; all-consuming-yet-never-satisfied wants; a brutal temper; an impotence to love or be loved; divided homes and divided lives; small-minded and lopsided pursuits; the vicious habit of depersonalizing everyone into a rival; uncontrolled and uncontrollable addictions; ugly parodies of community. I could go on.

This isn't the first time I have warned you, you know. If you use your freedom this way, you will not inherit God's kingdom.
— **GALATIANS** 5:19-21

Don't shuffle along, eyes to the ground, absorbed with the things right in front of you. Look up, and be alert to what is going on around Christ — that's where the action is. See things from *his* perspective.
— **COLOSSIANS** 3:2

Make sure you don't take things for granted and go slack in working for the common good; share what you have with others. God takes particular pleasure in acts of worship — a different kind of "sacrifice" — that take place in kitchen and workplace and on the streets.
— **HEBREWS** 13:16

People conceived and brought into life by God don't make a practice of sin. How could they? God's seed is deep within them, making them who they are. It's not in the nature of the God-begotten to practice and parade sin. — 1 **JOHN** 3:9

HAPPINESS

Day and night I'll stick with GOD;
    I've got a good thing going and I'm not letting go.

I'm happy from the inside out,
    and from the outside in, I'm firmly formed. — **PSALM** 16:8-9

[God] wraps you in goodness — beauty eternal.
He renews your youth — you're always young in his presence.
— **PSALM** 103:5

I inherited your book on living; it's mine forever —
    what a gift! And how happy it makes me! — **PSALM** 119:111

A pretentious, showy life is an empty life;
a plain and simple life is a full life. — PROVERBS 13:7

Laugh with your happy friends when they're happy; share tears when they're down. — ROMANS 12:15

Celebrate God all day, every day. I mean, *revel* in him!
— PHILIPPIANS 4:4

I'm just as happy with little as with much, with much as with little. I've found the recipe for being happy whether full or hungry, hands full or hands empty. — PHILIPPIANS 4:12

HEALTH

A cheerful disposition is good for your health;
gloom and doom leave you bone-tired. — PROVERBS 17:22

"The health of the apple tells the health of the tree. You must begin with your own life-giving lives." — LUKE 6:44

If anything, you have more concern for the lower parts than the higher. If you had to choose, wouldn't you prefer good digestion to full-bodied hair? — 1 CORINTHIANS 12:24

The way God designed our bodies is a model for understanding our lives together as a church: every part dependent on every other part, the parts we mention and the parts we don't, the parts we see and the parts we don't. If one part hurts, every other part is involved in the hurt, and in the healing. If one part flourishes, every other part enters into the exuberance.

You are Christ's body — that's who you are! You must never forget this. Only as you accept your part of that body does your "part" mean anything. You're familiar with some of the parts that God has formed in his church, which is his "body." — 1 CORINTHIANS 12:25-28

Workouts in the gymnasium are useful, but a disciplined life in God is far more so, making you fit both today and forever. You can count on this. Take it to heart. — 1 TIMOTHY 4:8-9

Are you hurting? Pray. Do you feel great? Sing. Are you sick? Call the church leaders together to pray and anoint you with oil in the name of the Master. Believing-prayer will heal you, and Jesus will put you on your feet. And if you've sinned, you'll be forgiven — healed inside and out.

Make this your common practice: Confess your sins to each other and pray for each other so that you can live together whole and healed. The prayer of a person living right with God is something powerful to be reckoned with. — JAMES 5:13-16

He used his servant body to carry our sins to the Cross so we could be rid of sin, free to live the right way. His wounds became your healing. — 1 PETER 2:24

I pray for good fortune in everything you do, and for your good health — that your everyday affairs prosper, as well as your soul!
— 3 JOHN 2

HONESTY

The integrity of the honest keeps them on track. — PROVERBS 11:3

An honest life shows respect for GOD;
    a degenerate life is a slap in his face. — PROVERBS 14:2

GOD cares about honesty in the workplace;
    your business is his business. — PROVERBS 16:11

Better to be poor and honest
    than a rich person no one can trust. — PROVERBS 19:1

God-loyal people, living honest lives,
    make it much easier for their children. — PROVERBS 20:7

We refuse to wear masks and play games. We don't maneuver and manipulate behind the scenes. And we don't twist God's Word to suit ourselves. Rather, we keep everything we do and say out in the open, the whole truth on display, so that those who want to can see and judge for themselves in the presence of God.

If our Message is obscure to anyone, it's not because we're holding back in any way. No, it's because these other people are looking or going the wrong way and refuse to give it serious attention. All they have eyes for is the fashionable god of darkness. They think he can give them what they want, and that they won't have to bother believing a Truth they can't see. They're stone-blind to the dayspring brightness of the Message that shines with Christ, who gives us the best picture of God we'll ever get. — 2 CORINTHIANS 4:2-4

God wants us to grow up, to know the whole truth and tell it in love — like Christ in everything. We take our lead from Christ, who is the source of everything we do. — EPHESIANS 4:15

HOPE

Be brave. Be strong. Don't give up.
Expect GOD to get here soon. — PSALM 31:24

Wait . . . for GOD. Wait with hope.
Hope now; hope always! — PSALM 131:3

"I'm a hostage here for hope, not doom." — ACTS 28:20

Waiting does not diminish us, any more than waiting diminishes a pregnant mother. We are enlarged in the waiting. — ROMANS 8:24

By no means do I count myself an expert in all of this, but I've got my eye on the goal, where God is beckoning us onward — to Jesus. I'm off and running, and I'm not turning back. — PHILIPPIANS 3:13-14

The lines of purpose in your lives never grow slack, tightly tied as they are to your future in heaven, kept taut by hope. — COLOSSIANS 1:5

When God wanted to guarantee his promises, he gave his word, a rock-solid guarantee — God *can't* break his word. And because his word cannot change, the promise is likewise unchangeable.

 We who have run for our very lives to God have every reason to grab the promised hope with both hands and never let go. It's an unbreakable spiritual lifeline, reaching past all appearances right to the very presence of God. — HEBREWS 6:17-19

JEALOUSY

Jealousy detonates rage in a cheated husband;
 wild for revenge, he won't make allowances. — PROVERBS 6:34

Don't envy bad people;
 don't even want to be around them. — PROVERBS 24:1

We're blasted by anger and swamped by rage,
 but who can survive jealousy? — PROVERBS 27:4

Since this is the kind of life we have chosen, the life of the Spirit, let us make sure that we do not just hold it as an idea in our heads or a sentiment in our hearts, but work out its implications in every detail of our lives. That means we will not compare ourselves with each other as if one of us were better and another worse. We have far more interesting things to do with our lives. Each of us is an original.

— **GALATIANS** 5:25-26

Whenever you're trying to look better than others or get the better of others, things fall apart and everyone ends up at the others' throats.

— **JAMES** 3:16

JESUS

"She will bring a son to birth, and when she does, you, Joseph, will name him Jesus — 'God saves' — because he will save his people from their sins." — **MATTHEW** 1:21

"Don't be upset, and don't let all these doubting questions take over. Look at my hands; look at my feet — it's really me. Touch me. Look me over from head to toe. A ghost doesn't have muscle and bone like this." As he said this, he showed them his hands and feet.

— **LUKE** 24:38-40

Jesus said, "I am the Road, also the Truth, also the Life. No one gets to the Father apart from me. If you really knew me, you would know my

Father as well. From now on, you do know him. You've even seen him!"
— JOHN 14:6-7

We look at this Son and see the God who cannot be seen. We look at this Son and see God's original purpose in everything created. For everything, absolutely everything, above and below, visible and invisible, rank after rank after rank of angels — *everything* got started in him and finds its purpose in him. He was there before any of it came into existence and holds it all together right up to this moment. And when it comes to the church, he organizes and holds it together, like a head does a body.

He was supreme in the beginning and — leading the resurrection parade — he is supreme in the end. From beginning to end he's there, towering far above everything, everyone. So spacious is he, so roomy, that everything of God finds its proper place in him without crowding. Not only that, but all the broken and dislocated pieces of the universe — people and things, animals and atoms — get properly fixed and fit together in vibrant harmonies, all because of his death, his blood that poured down from the Cross. — COLOSSIANS 1:15-20

Going through a long line of prophets, God has been addressing our ancestors in different ways for centuries. Recently he spoke to us directly through his Son. By his Son, God created the world in the beginning, and it will all belong to the Son at the end. This Son perfectly mirrors God, and is stamped with God's nature. He holds everything together by what he says — powerful words!

After he finished the sacrifice for sins, the Son took his honored place high in the heavens right alongside God, far higher than any angel in rank and rule. Did God ever say to an angel, "You're my Son; today I celebrate you"? Or, "I'm his Father, he's my Son"? When he presents his honored Son to the world, he says, "All angels must worship him."

— HEBREWS 1:1-6

LAZINESS

You lazy fool, look at an ant.
    Watch it closely; let it teach you a thing or two. — PROVERBS 6:6

A lazy employee will give you nothing but trouble. — PROVERBS 10:26

The diligent find freedom in their work;
    the lazy are oppressed by work. — PROVERBS 12:24

A lazy life is an empty life. — PROVERBS 12:27

"Stay alert, be in prayer, so you don't enter the danger zone without even knowing it. Don't be naive. Part of you is eager, ready for anything in God; but another part is as lazy as an old dog sleeping by the fire." — MARK 14:38

Did you used to make ends meet by stealing? Well, no more! Get an honest job so that you can help others who can't work.

— EPHESIANS 4:28

Stay calm; mind your own business; do your own job. You've heard all this from us before, but a reminder never hurts. We want you living in a way that will command the respect of outsiders, not lying around sponging off your friends. — 1 THESSALONIANS 4:11-12

Our counsel is that you warn the freeloaders to get a move on. Gently encourage the stragglers, and reach out for the exhausted, pulling them to their feet. Be patient with each person, attentive to individual needs. — 1 THESSALONIANS 5:14

Our orders — backed up by the Master, Jesus — are to refuse to have anything to do with those among you who are lazy and refuse to work the way we taught you. Don't permit them to freeload on the rest. We showed you how to pull your weight when we were with you, so get on with it. We didn't sit around on our hands expecting others to take care of us. — 2 THESSALONIANS 3:6-8

Don't you remember the rule we had when we lived with you? "If you don't work, you don't eat." And now we're getting reports that a bunch of lazy good-for-nothings are taking advantage of you. This must not be tolerated. We command them to get to work immediately — no excuses, no arguments — and earn their own keep.
— 2 THESSALONIANS 3:10-12

Don't drag your feet. Be like those who stay the course with committed faith and then get everything promised to them. — HEBREWS 6:12

Who out there has a lust for life?
Can't wait each day to come upon beauty? — PSALM 34:12

Don't put your life in the hands of experts
who know nothing of life, of *salvation* life. — PSALM 146:3

A life devoted to things is a dead life, a stump;
a God-shaped life is a flourishing tree. — PROVERBS 11:28

A pretentious, showy life is an empty life;
a plain and simple life is a full life. — PROVERBS 13:7

An honest life shows respect for GOD;
a degenerate life is a slap in his face. — PROVERBS 14:2

An undisciplined, self-willed life is puny;
an obedient, God-willed life is spacious. — PROVERBS 15:32

It pays to take life seriously;
things work out when you trust in GOD. — PROVERBS 16:20

GOD is in charge of human life,
   watching and examining us inside and out. — **PROVERBS** 20:27

"Steep your life in God-reality, God-initiative, God-provisions. Don't worry about missing out. You'll find all your everyday human concerns will be met." — **MATTHEW** 6:33

[Jesus said,] "First things first. Your business is life, not death. Follow me. Pursue life." — **MATTHEW** 8:22

"Don't set people up as experts over your life, letting them tell you what to do. Save that authority for God; let *him* tell you what to do."
— **MATTHEW** 23:9

"Give away your life; you'll find life given back, but not merely given back — given back with bonus and blessing. Giving, not getting, is the way. Generosity begets generosity." — **LUKE** 6:38

"Keep your life as well-lighted as your best-lighted room."
— **LUKE** 11:36

"Life is not defined by what you have, even when you have a lot."
— **LUKE** 12:15

"Put your mind on your life with God. The way to life — to God! — is vigorous and requires your total attention." — LUKE 13:24

"If you grasp and cling to life on your terms, you'll lose it, but if you let that life go, you'll get life on God's terms." — LUKE 17:33

Work hard for sin your whole life and your pension is death. But God's gift is real life, eternal life, delivered by Jesus, our Master. — ROMANS 6:23

Each of you must take responsibility for doing the creative best you can with your own life. — GALATIANS 6:5

Your old life is dead. Your new life, which is your *real* life — even though invisible to spectators — is with Christ in God. He is your life. — COLOSSIANS 3:3

Your life is a journey you must travel with a deep consciousness of God. It cost God plenty to get you out of that dead-end, empty-headed life you grew up in. — 1 PETER 1:17-18

Your new life is not like your old life. Your old birth came from mortal sperm; your new birth comes from God's living Word. Just think: a life conceived by God himself! — 1 PETER 1:23

If we claim that we experience a shared life with him and continue to stumble around in the dark, we're obviously lying through our teeth — we're not *living* what we claim. — 1 JOHN 1:6

If someone claims, "I know him well!" but doesn't keep his commandments, he's obviously a liar. His life doesn't match his words.
— 1 JOHN 2:4

Anyone who claims to be intimate with God ought to live the same kind of life Jesus lived. — 1 JOHN 2:6

LONELINESS

Look at me and help me!
I'm all alone and in big trouble. — PSALM 25:16

Look right, look left —
    there's not a soul who cares what happens!
I'm up against it, with no exit —
    bereft, left alone. — PSALM 142:4

With the crowd dispersed, Jesus climbed the mountain so he could be by himself and pray. He stayed there alone, late into the night.
— MATTHEW 14:23

[Jesus said,] "I will not leave you orphaned. I'm coming back."
— JOHN 14:18

Real religion, the kind that passes muster before God the Father, is this: Reach out to the homeless and loveless in their plight, and guard against corruption from the godless world. — JAMES 1:27

When you extend hospitality to Christian brothers and sisters, even when they are strangers, you make the faith visible. — 3 JOHN 5

LOVE

I can always count on you —
God, my dependable love. — PSALM 59:17

Better a bread crust shared in love
    than a slab of prime rib served in hate. — PROVERBS 15:17

Lots of people claim to be loyal and loving,
    but where on earth can you find one? — PROVERBS 20:6

[Jesus said,] "You're familiar with the old written law, 'Love your friend,' and its unwritten companion, 'Hate your enemy.' I'm challenging that. I'm telling you to love your enemies. Let them bring out the best in you, not the worst. When someone gives you a hard time, respond with the energies of prayer, for then you are working out of your true selves, your God-created selves." — **MATTHEW** 5:43-45

"'Love the Lord your God with all your passion and prayer and intelligence.' This is the most important, the first on any list. But there is a second to set alongside it: 'Love others as well as you love yourself.' These two commands are pegs; everything in God's Law and the Prophets hangs from them." — **MATTHEW** 22:37-40

"Anyone who holds on to life just as it is destroys that life. But if you let it go, reckless in your love, you'll have it forever, real and eternal." — **JOHN** 12:25

"If you lived on the world's terms, the world would love you as one of its own. But since I picked you to live on God's terms and no longer on the world's terms, the world is going to hate you." — **JOHN** 15:19

God put his love on the line for us by offering his Son in sacrificial death while we were of no use whatever to him. — **ROMANS** 5:8

Do you think anyone is going to be able to drive a wedge between us and Christ's love for us? There is no way! Not trouble, not hard times, not hatred, not hunger, not homelessness, not bullying threats, not backstabbing, not even the worst sins listed in Scripture . . . nothing—

nothing living or dead, angelic or demonic, today or tomorrow, high or low, thinkable or unthinkable — absolutely *nothing* can get between us and God's love because of the way that Jesus our Master has embraced us. — ROMANS 8:35,38-39

Love from the center of who you are; don't fake it. Run for dear life from evil; hold on for dear life to good. Be good friends who love deeply. — ROMANS 12:9-10

No matter what I say, what I believe, and what I do, I'm bankrupt without love.

> Love never gives up.
> Love cares more for others than for self.
> Love doesn't want what it doesn't have.
> Love doesn't strut,
> Doesn't have a swelled head,
> Doesn't force itself on others,
> Isn't always "me first,"
> Doesn't fly off the handle,
> Doesn't keep score of the sins of others,
> Doesn't revel when others grovel,
> Takes pleasure in the flowering of truth,
> Puts up with anything,
> Trusts God always,
> Always looks for the best,
> Never looks back,
> But keeps going to the end.
> Love never dies. — 1 CORINTHIANS 13:3-8

I ask [the Father] that with both feet planted firmly on love, you'll be able to take in with all Christians the extravagant dimensions of Christ's love. Reach out and experience the breadth! Test its length! Plumb the depths! Rise to the heights! Live full lives, full in the fullness of God.
— EPHESIANS 3:17-19

Watch what God does, and then you do it, like children who learn proper behavior from their parents. Mostly what God does is love you. Keep company with him and learn a life of love. Observe how Christ loved us. His love was not cautious but extravagant. He didn't love in order to get something from us but to give everything of himself to us. Love like that. — EPHESIANS 5:1-2

This is my prayer: that your love will flourish and that you will not only love much but well. Learn to love appropriately. You need to use your head and test your feelings so that your love is sincere and intelligent, not sentimental gush. Live a lover's life, circumspect and exemplary, a life Jesus will be proud of. — PHILIPPIANS 1:9-10

The whole point of what we're urging is simply *love* — love uncontaminated by self-interest and counterfeit faith, a life open to God.
— 1 TIMOTHY 1:5

Most of all, love each other as if your life depended on it. Love makes up for practically anything. — 1 PETER 4:8

Don't love the world's ways. Don't love the world's goods. Love of the world squeezes out love for the Father. — 1 JOHN 2:15

Anyone who doesn't love is as good as dead. . . .

This is how we've come to understand and experience love: Christ sacrificed his life for us. This is why we ought to live sacrificially for our fellow believers, and not just be out for ourselves. If you see some brother or sister in need and have the means to do something about it but turn a cold shoulder and do nothing, what happens to God's love? It disappears. And you made it disappear.

My dear children, let's not just talk about love; let's practice real love. — 1 JOHN 3:14, 16-18

My beloved friends, let us continue to love each other since love comes from God. Everyone who loves is born of God and experiences a relationship with God. The person who refuses to love doesn't know the first thing about God, because God *is* love — so you can't know him if you don't love. This is how God showed his love for us: God sent his only Son into the world so we might live through him. . . . If God loved us like this, we certainly ought to love each other. No one has seen God, ever. But if we love one another, God dwells deeply within us, and his love becomes complete in us — perfect love!

— 1 JOHN 4:7-9,11-12

Loving God includes loving people. You've got to love both.

— 1 JOHN 4:21

Good character is the best insurance;
> crooks get trapped in their sinful lust. — **PROVERBS** 1 1 : 6

[Jesus said,] "You know the next commandment pretty well, too: 'Don't go to bed with another's spouse.' But don't think you've preserved your virtue simply by staying out of bed. Your *heart* can be corrupted by lust even quicker than your *body*. Those leering looks you think nobody notices — they also corrupt." — **MATTHEW** 5 : 2 7 - 2 8

"Using the legalities of divorce
> as a cover for lust is adultery.

Using the legalities of marriage
> as a cover for lust is adultery." — **LUKE** 1 6 : 1 8

Since, then, we do not have the excuse of ignorance, everything — and I do mean everything — connected with that old way of life has to go. It's rotten through and through. Get rid of it! And then take on an entirely new way of life — a God-fashioned life, a life renewed from the inside and working itself into your conduct as God accurately reproduces his character in you. — **EPHESIANS** 4 : 2 2 - 2 4

Don't allow love to turn into lust, setting off a downhill slide into sexual promiscuity, filthy practices, or bullying greed. — **EPHESIANS** 5 : 3

Be content with obscurity, like Christ.

And that means killing off everything connected with the way of death: sexual promiscuity, impurity, lust, doing whatever you feel like whenever you feel like it, and grabbing whatever attracts your fancy. That's a life shaped by things and feelings instead of by God.
— COLOSSIANS 3:4-5

Lust for money brings trouble and nothing but trouble. Going down that path, some lose their footing in the faith completely and live to regret it bitterly ever after. — 1 TIMOTHY 6:10

It wasn't so long ago that we ourselves were stupid and stubborn, dupes of sin, ordered every which way by our glands, going around with a chip on our shoulder, hated and hating back. But when God, our kind and loving Savior God, stepped in, he saved us from all that. It was all his doing; we had nothing to do with it. He gave us a good bath, and we came out of it new people, washed inside and out by the Holy Spirit. — TITUS 3:3-5

Lust gets pregnant, and has a baby: sin! Sin grows up to adulthood, and becomes a real killer. — JAMES 1:15

Where do you think all these appalling wars and quarrels come from? Do you think they just happen? Think again. They come about because you want your own way, and fight for it deep inside yourselves. You lust for what you don't have and are willing to kill to get it. You want what isn't yours and will risk violence to get your hands on it.

You wouldn't think of just asking God for it, would you? And why not? Because you know you'd be asking for what you have no right to. You're spoiled children, each wanting your own way.

You're cheating on God. If all you want is your own way, flirting with the world every chance you get, you end up enemies of God and his way. — JAMES 4:1-4

So let God work his will in you. Yell a loud no to the Devil and watch him scamper. Say a quiet yes to God and he'll be there in no time. Quit dabbling in sin. Purify your inner life. Quit playing the field. — JAMES 4:7-8

This world is not your home, so don't make yourselves cozy in it. Don't indulge your ego at the expense of your soul. — 1 PETER 2:11

We were given absolutely terrific promises to pass on to you — your tickets to participation in the life of God after you turned your back on a world corrupted by lust. — 2 PETER 1:4

Practically everything that goes on in the world — wanting your own way, wanting everything for yourself, wanting to appear important — has nothing to do with the Father. It just isolates you from him. The world and all its wanting, wanting, wanting is on the way out — but whoever does what God wants is set for eternity. — 1 JOHN 2:16-17

LYING

How long will you lust after lies?
How long will you live crazed by illusion? — **PSALM** 4:2

Don't talk out of both sides of your mouth;
    avoid careless banter, white lies, and gossip. — **PROVERBS** 4:24

Truth lasts;
    lies are here today, gone tomorrow. — **PROVERBS** 12:19

The person who tells lies gets caught;
    the person who spreads rumors is ruined. — **PROVERBS** 19:9

God's angry displeasure erupts as acts of human mistrust and wrongdoing and lying accumulate, as people try to put a shroud over truth.
— **ROMANS** 1:18

God keeps his word even when the whole world is lying through its
teeth. — **ROMANS** 3:4

Tell your neighbor the truth. In Christ's body we're all connected to
each other, after all. When you lie to others, you end up lying to yourself. — **EPHESIANS** 4:25

But you know better now, so make sure it's all gone for good: bad temper, irritability, meanness, profanity, dirty talk.

Don't lie to one another. You're done with that old life. It's like a filthy set of ill-fitting clothes you've stripped off and put in the fire. Now you're dressed in a new wardrobe. Every item of your new way of life is custom-made by the Creator, with his label on it. All the old fashions are now obsolete.

— COLOSSIANS 3:8-10

These liars have lied so well and for so long that they've lost their capacity for truth. — 1 TIMOTHY 4:2

If we claim that we experience a shared life with him and continue to stumble around in the dark, we're obviously lying through our teeth — we're not living what we claim. — 1 JOHN 1:6

MARRIAGE

House and land are handed down from parents,
  but a congenial spouse comes straight from GOD.
— PROVERBS 19:14

A good woman is hard to find,
  and worth far more than diamonds.
Her husband trusts her without reserve,
  and never has reason to regret it.

Never spiteful, she treats him generously
     all her life long. . . .
When she speaks she has something worthwhile to say,
     and she always says it kindly.
She keeps an eye on everyone in her household,
     and keeps them all busy and productive.
Her children respect and bless her;
     her husband joins in with words of praise.
— **PROVERBS** 31:10-12,26-28

Jesus said, "Not everyone is mature enough to live a married life. It requires a certain aptitude and grace. Marriage isn't for everyone. Some, from birth seemingly, never give marriage a thought. Others never get asked — or accepted. And some decide not to get married for kingdom reasons. But if you're capable of growing into the largeness of marriage, do it." — **MATTHEW** 19:11-12

"A man leaves father and mother, and in marriage he becomes one flesh with a woman — no longer two individuals, but forming a new unity. Because God created this organic union of the two sexes, no one should desecrate his art by cutting them apart." — **MARK** 10:7-9

If [you] can't manage your desires and emotions, [you] should by all means go ahead and get married. The difficulties of marriage are preferable by far to a sexually tortured life as a single. — **1 CORINTHIANS** 7:9

If you are a man with a wife who is not a believer but who still wants to live with you, hold on to her. If you are a woman with a husband who is not a believer but he wants to live with you, hold on to him. The unbelieving husband shares to an extent in the holiness of his wife, and the unbelieving wife is likewise touched by the holiness of her husband. Otherwise, your children would be left out; as it is, they also are included in the spiritual purposes of God. — 1 CORINTHIANS 7:12-14

A wife must stay with her husband as long as he lives. If he dies, she is free to marry anyone she chooses. She will, of course, want to marry a believer and have the blessing of the Master.
— 1 CORINTHIANS 7:39

Don't become partners with those who reject God. How can you make a partnership out of right and wrong? That's not partnership; that's war. Is light best friends with dark? — 2 CORINTHIANS 6:14

Out of respect for Christ, be courteously reverent to one another.

Wives, understand and support your husbands in ways that show your support for Christ. The husband provides leadership to his wife the way Christ does to his church, not by domineering but by cherishing. So just as the church submits to Christ as he exercises such leadership, wives should likewise submit to their husbands.

Husbands, go all out in your love for your wives, exactly as Christ did for the church — a love marked by giving, not getting. Christ's love makes the church whole. His words evoke her beauty. Everything he does and says is designed to bring the best out of her, dressing her in dazzling white silk, radiant with holiness. And that is how husbands ought to love their wives. They're really doing themselves a favor — since they're already "one" in marriage. — **EPHESIANS** 5:21-28

Wives, understand and support your husbands by submitting to them in ways that honor the Master.

Husbands, go all out in love for your wives. Don't take advantage of them. — **COLOSSIANS** 3:18-19

Honor marriage, and guard the sacredness of sexual intimacy between wife and husband. God draws a firm line against casual and illicit sex. — **HEBREWS** 13:4

The same goes for you wives: Be good wives to your husbands, responsive to their needs. There are husbands who, indifferent as they are to any words about God, will be captivated by your life of holy beauty. What matters is not your outer appearance — the styling of your hair, the jewelry you wear, the cut of your clothes — but your inner disposition.

Cultivate inner beauty, the gentle, gracious kind that God delights in....

The same goes for you husbands: Be good husbands to your wives. Honor them, delight in them. As women they lack some of your advantages. But in the new life of God's grace, you're equals. Treat your wives, then, as equals so your prayers don't run aground.

— **1 PETER** 3:1-4,7

MATERIALISM

Honor GOD with everything you own;
> give him the first and the best. — **PROVERBS** 3:9

A life devoted to things is a dead life, a stump;
> a God-shaped life is a flourishing tree. — **PROVERBS** 11:28

The rich can be sued for everything they have,
> but the poor are free of such threats. — **PROVERBS** 13:8

Better to be poor and honest
> than a rich person no one can trust. — **PROVERBS** 19:1

"Don't hoard treasure down here where it gets eaten by moths and corroded by rust or — worse! — stolen by burglars. Stockpile treasure in heaven, where it's safe from moth and rust and burglars. It's obvious, isn't it? The place where your treasure is, is the place you will most want to be, and end up being." — **MATTHEW** 6:19-21

Jesus looked him hard in the eye — and loved him! He said, "There's one thing left: Go sell whatever you own and give it to the poor. All your wealth will then be heavenly wealth. And come follow me."

The man's face clouded over. This was the last thing he expected to hear, and he walked off with a heavy heart. He was holding on tight to a lot of things, and not about to let go.

Looking at his disciples, Jesus said, "Do you have any idea how difficult it is for people who 'have it all' to enter God's kingdom?"
— **MARK** 10:21-23

"Life is not defined by what you have, even when you have a lot."
— **LUKE** 12:15

"Is there anyone here who, planning to build a new house, doesn't first sit down and figure the cost so you'll know if you can complete it?"
— **LUKE** 14:28

Don't be obsessed with getting more material things. Be relaxed with what you have. Since God assured us, "I'll never let you down, never walk off and leave you." — **HEBREWS** 13:5

A final word to you arrogant rich: Take some lessons in lament. You'll need buckets for the tears when the crash comes upon you. Your money is corrupt and your fine clothes stink. Your greedy luxuries are a cancer in your gut, destroying your life from within. You thought you were piling up wealth. What you've piled up is judgment. — **JAMES** 5:1-3

The world and all its wanting, wanting, wanting is on the way out — but whoever does what God wants is set for eternity. — 1 **JOHN** 2:17

If you see some brother or sister in need and have the means to do something about it but turn a cold shoulder and do nothing, what happens to God's love? It disappears. And you made it disappear.
— 1 JOHN 3:17

MONEY

Mercy to the needy is a loan to GOD,
and GOD pays back those loans in full. — PROVERBS 19:17

If you stop your ears to the cries of the poor,
your cries will go unheard, unanswered. — PROVERBS 21:13

Don't gamble on the pot of gold at the end of the rainbow,
hocking your house against a lucky chance. — PROVERBS 22:26

"You can't worship two gods at once. Loving one god, you'll end up hating the other. Adoration of one feeds contempt for the other. You can't worship God and Money both." — MATTHEW 6:24

Sitting across from the offering box, [Jesus] was observing how the crowd tossed money in for the collection. Many of the rich were making large contributions. One poor widow came up and put in two small coins — a measly two cents. Jesus called his disciples over and said, "The truth is that this poor widow gave more to the collection than all the others put together. All the others gave what they'll never miss; she gave extravagantly what she couldn't afford — she gave her all." — MARK 12:41-44

You are familiar with the generosity of our Master, Jesus Christ. Rich as he was, he gave it all away for us — in one stroke he became poor and we became rich. — 2 CORINTHIANS 8:9

Lust for money brings trouble and nothing but trouble. Going down that path, some lose their footing in the faith completely and live to regret it bitterly ever after. — 1 TIMOTHY 6:10

Tell those rich in this world's wealth to quit being so full of themselves and so obsessed with money, which is here today and gone tomorrow. Tell them to go after God, who piles on all the riches we could ever manage — to do good, to be rich in helping others, to be extravagantly generous. If they do that, they'll build a treasury that will last, gaining life that is truly life. — 1 TIMOTHY 6:17-19

MOTIVES

Examine me, GOD, from head to foot,
     order your battery of tests.
Make sure I'm fit
     inside and out. — PSALM 26:2

A bad motive can't achieve a good end;
>   double-talk brings you double trouble. — **PROVERBS** 17:20

We justify our actions by appearances;
>   GOD examines our motives. — **PROVERBS** 21:2

Mixed motives twist life into tangles;
>   pure motives take you straight down the road. — **PROVERBS** 21:8

The fear of human opinion disables;
>   trusting in GOD protects you from that. — **PROVERBS** 29:25

"You're blessed when you get your inside world—your mind and heart—put right. Then you can see God in the outside world."
— **MATTHEW** 5:8

"Be especially careful when you are trying to be good so that you don't make a performance out of it. It might be good theater, but the God who made you won't be applauding.

"When you do something for someone else, don't call attention to yourself. You've seen them in action, I'm sure—'playactors' I call them—treating prayer meeting and street corner alike as a stage, acting compassionate as long as someone is watching, playing to the crowds. They get applause, true, but that's all they get. When you help someone out, don't think about how it looks. Just do it—quietly and unobtrusively. That is the way your God, who conceived you in love, working behind the scenes, helps you out." — MATTHEW 6:1-4

[Jesus said,] "If your first concern is to look after yourself, you'll never find yourself. But if you forget about yourself and look to me, you'll find both yourself and me." — MATTHEW 10:39

"The health of the apple tells the health of the tree. You must begin with your own life-giving lives. It's who you are, not what you say and do, that counts. Your true being brims over into true words and deeds." — LUKE 6:44-45

It matters very little to me what you think of me, even less where I rank in popular opinion. I don't even rank myself. Comparisons in these matters are pointless. . . .

So don't get ahead of the Master and jump to conclusions with your judgments before all the evidence is in. When he comes, he will bring out in the open and place in evidence all kinds of things we never even dreamed of — inner motives and purposes and prayers. Only then will any one of us get to hear the "Well done!" of God.

— 1 CORINTHIANS 4:3,5

Do everything readily and cheerfully — no bickering, no second-guessing allowed! Go out into the world uncorrupted, a breath of fresh air in this squalid and polluted society. Provide people with a glimpse of good living and of the living God. — PHILIPPIANS 2:14-15

"I x-ray every motive and make sure you get what's coming to you."
— **REVELATION** 2:23

OBEDIENCE

You're blessed when you stay on course,
    walking steadily on the road revealed by GOD.
You're blessed when you follow his directions,
    doing your best to find him.
That's right — you don't go off on your own;
    you walk straight along the road he set. — **PSALM** 119:1-3

[Jesus said,] "Knowing the correct password — saying 'Master, Master,' for instance — isn't going to get you anywhere with me. What is required is serious obedience — doing what my Father wills."
— **MATTHEW** 7:21

"Obedience is thicker than blood. The person who obeys my heavenly Father's will is my brother and sister and mother." — **MATTHEW** 12:50

[Jesus said,] "If you love me, show it by doing what I've told you."
— **JOHN** 14:15

Merely hearing God's law is a waste of your time if you don't do what he commands. Doing, not hearing, is what makes the difference with God. — **ROMANS** 2:13

We know very well that we are not set right with God by rule-keeping but only through personal faith in Jesus Christ. How do we know? We tried it — and we had the best system of rules the world has ever seen! Convinced that no human being can please God by self-improvement, we believed in Jesus as the Messiah so that we might be set right before God by trusting in the Messiah, not by trying to be good. . . .

Is it not clear to you that to go back to that old rule-keeping, peer-pleasing religion would be an abandonment of everything personal and free in my relationship with God? I refuse to do that, to repudiate God's grace. If a living relationship with God could come by rule-keeping, then Christ died unnecessarily. — GALATIANS 2:16,21

Exercise your freedom by serving God, not by breaking the rules.
— 1 PETER 2:16

The reality test on whether or not we love God's children is this: Do we love God? Do we keep his commands? The proof that we love God comes when we keep his commandments and they are not at all troublesome. — 1 JOHN 5:2-3

PATIENCE

Stay with GOD!
Take heart. Don't quit.
I'll say it again:
Stay with GOD. — PSALM 27:14

Patient persistence pierces through indifference;
  gentle speech breaks down rigid defenses. — PROVERBS 25:15

"Staying with it — that's what God requires. Stay with it to the end. You won't be sorry, and you'll be saved." — MATTHEW 24:13

We continue to shout our praise even when we're hemmed in with troubles, because we know how troubles can develop passionate patience in us, and how that patience in turn forges the tempered steel of virtue, keeping us alert for whatever God will do next. — ROMANS 5:3-4

Waiting does not diminish us, any more than waiting diminishes a pregnant mother. We are enlarged in the waiting. We, of course, don't see what is enlarging us. But the longer we wait, the larger we become, and the more joyful our expectancy. — ROMANS 8:24-25

We pray that you'll have the strength to stick it out over the long haul — not the grim strength of gritting your teeth but the glory-strength God gives. It is strength that endures the unendurable and spills over into joy. — COLOSSIANS 1:11

If we can only keep our grip on the sure thing we started out with, we're in this with Christ for the long haul. — HEBREWS 3:14

You need to stick it out, staying with God's plan so you'll be there for the promised completion. — **HEBREWS** 10:36

Wait patiently for the Master's Arrival. You see farmers do this all the time, waiting for their valuable crops to mature, patiently letting the rain do its slow but sure work. Be patient like that. Stay steady and strong. The Master could arrive at any time. — **JAMES** 5:7-8

What a gift life is to those who stay the course! You've heard, of course, of Job's staying power, and you know how God brought it all together for him at the end. That's because God cares, cares right down to the last detail. — **JAMES** 5:11

PEACE

At day's end I'm ready for sound sleep,
For you, GOD, have put my life back together. — **PSALM** 4:8

A meal of bread and water in contented peace
is better than a banquet spiced with quarrels. — **PROVERBS** 17:1

"You're blessed when you can show people how to cooperate instead of compete or fight. That's when you discover who you really are, and your place in God's family." — **MATTHEW** 5:9

[Jesus said,] "I'm leaving you well and whole. That's my parting gift to you. Peace. I don't leave you the way you're used to being left — feeling abandoned, bereft. So don't be upset. Don't be distraught."
— JOHN 14:27

"I've told you all this so that trusting me, you will be unshakable and assured, deeply at peace. In this godless world you will continue to experience difficulties. But take heart! I've conquered the world."
— JOHN 16:33

Don't hit back; discover beauty in everyone. If you've got it in you, get along with everybody. — ROMANS 12:17-18

Be a good citizen. All governments are under God. Insofar as there is peace and order, it's God's order. So live responsibly as a citizen.
— ROMANS 13:1

What happens when we live God's way? He brings gifts into our lives, much the same way that fruit appears in an orchard — things like affection for others, exuberance about life, serenity. We develop a willingness to stick with things, a sense of compassion in the heart, and a conviction that a basic holiness permeates things and people. We find ourselves involved in loyal commitments. — GALATIANS 5:22

Let the peace of Christ keep you in tune with each other, in step with each other. None of this going off and doing your own thing. And cultivate thankfulness. — COLOSSIANS 3:15

Real wisdom, God's wisdom, begins with a holy life and is characterized by getting along with others. It is gentle and reasonable, overflowing with mercy and blessings, not hot one day and cold the next, not two-faced. You can develop a healthy, robust community that lives right with God and enjoy its results only if you do the hard work of getting along with each other, treating each other with dignity and honor. — JAMES 3:17-18

PLANNING

God's plan for the world stands up,
 all his designs are made to last. — PSALM 33:11

There's a way of life that looks harmless enough;
 look again — it leads straight to hell. — PROVERBS 14:12

Refuse good advice and watch your plans fail;
 take good counsel and watch them succeed. — PROVERBS 15:22

Mortals make elaborate plans,
 but God has the last word. — PROVERBS 16:1

We plan the way we want to live,
>   but only GOD makes us able to live it. — **PROVERBS** 16:9

Jesus Christ rescued us from this evil world we're in by offering himself as a sacrifice for our sins. God's plan is that we all experience that rescue. — **GALATIANS** 1:4

When you attempt to live by your own religious plans and projects, you are cut off from Christ, you fall out of grace. — **GALATIANS** 5:4

And now I have a word for you who brashly announce, "Today — at the latest, tomorrow — we're off to such and such a city for the year. We're going to start a business and make a lot of money." You don't know the first thing about tomorrow. You're nothing but a wisp of fog, catching a brief bit of sun before disappearing. Instead, make it a habit to say, "If the Master wills it and we're still alive, we'll do this or that." — **JAMES** 4:13-15

PRAYER

Keep company with GOD,
>   get in on the best. — **PSALM** 37:4

GOD's there, listening for all who pray,
>   for all who pray and mean it. — **PSALM** 145:18

[Jesus said,] "Find a quiet, secluded place so you won't be tempted to role-play before God. Just be there as simply and honestly as you can manage. The focus will shift from you to God, and you will begin to sense his grace.

"The world is full of so-called prayer warriors who are prayer-ignorant. They're full of formulas and programs and advice, peddling techniques for getting what you want from God. Don't fall for that nonsense. This is your Father you are dealing with, and he knows better than you what you need. . . .

"In prayer there is a connection between what God does and what you do. You can't get forgiveness from God, for instance, without also forgiving others. If you refuse to do your part, you cut yourself off from God's part." — MATTHEW 6:6-8,14-15

At about that same time [Jesus] climbed a mountain to pray. He was there all night in prayer before God. — LUKE 6:12

"Don't bargain with God. Be direct. Ask for what you need. This is not a cat-and-mouse, hide-and-seek game we're in." — LUKE 11:10

[Jesus said,] "If you make yourselves at home with me and my words are at home in you, you can be sure that whatever you ask will be listened to and acted upon." — JOHN 15:7

Don't fret or worry. Instead of worrying, pray. Let petitions and praises shape your worries into prayers, letting God know your concerns.

Before you know it, a sense of God's wholeness, everything coming together for good, will come and settle you down. It's wonderful what happens when Christ displaces worry at the center of your life.
— PHILIPPIANS 4:6-7

Pray all the time. — 1 THESSALONIANS 5:17

PRIDE

First pride, then the crash —
    the bigger the ego, the harder the fall. — PROVERBS 16:18

Don't call attention to yourself;
    let others do that for you. — PROVERBS 27:2

If you think you know it all, you're a fool for sure;
    real survivors learn wisdom from others. — PROVERBS 28:26

"Do you want to stand out? Then step down. Be a servant. If you puff yourself up, you'll get the wind knocked out of you. But if you're content to simply be yourself, your life will count for plenty."
— MATTHEW 23:11-12

[Jesus] sat down and summoned the Twelve. "So you want first place? Then take the last place. Be the servant of all." — MARK 9:35

"If you walk around with your nose in the air, you're going to end up flat on your face. But if you're content to be simply yourself, you will become more than yourself." — LUKE 14:11

So Jesus spoke to them: "You are masters at making yourselves look good in front of others, but God knows what's behind the appearance." — LUKE 16:15

Looking back over what has been accomplished and what I have observed, I must say I am most pleased — in the context of Jesus, I'd even say proud, but only in that context. — ROMANS 15:17

Take a good look, friends, at who you were when you got called into this life. I don't see many of "the brightest and the best" among you, not many influential, not many from high-society families. Isn't it obvious that God deliberately chose men and women that the culture overlooks and exploits and abuses, chose these "nobodies" to expose the hollow pretensions of the "somebodies"? That makes it quite clear that none of you can get by with blowing your own horn before God. — 1 CORINTHIANS 1:26-29

We are servants of Christ, not his masters. We are guides into God's most sublime secrets, not security guards posted to protect them. — 1 CORINTHIANS 4:1

Who do you know that really knows you, knows your heart? And even if they did, is there anything they would discover in you that you could take credit for? Isn't everything you have and everything you are sheer gifts from God? So what's the point of all this comparing and competing? You already have all you need. You already have more access to God than you can handle. — 1 CORINTHIANS 4:7-8

What you say about yourself means nothing in God's work. It's what God says about you that makes the difference. — 2 CORINTHIANS 10:18

That means we will not compare ourselves with each other as if one of us were better and another worse. We have far more interesting things to do with our lives. Each of us is an original. — GALATIANS 5:26

Be content with who you are, and don't put on airs. God's strong hand is on you; he'll promote you at the right time. — 1 PETER 5:6

Anyone who gets so progressive in his thinking that he walks out on the teaching of Christ, walks out on God. — 2 JOHN 9

PROMISES

GOD promises to love me all day,
 sing songs all through the night!
 My life is God's prayer. — PSALM 42:8

Do for GOD what you said you'd do
he is, after all, your God. — **PSALM** 76:11

"Don't say anything you don't mean. This counsel is embedded deep in our traditions. You only make things worse when you lay down a smoke screen of pious talk, saying, 'I'll pray for you,' and never doing it, or saying, 'God be with you,' and not meaning it. You don't make your words true by embellishing them with religious lace. In making your speech sound more religious, it becomes less true. Just say 'yes' and 'no.' When you manipulate words to get your own way, you go wrong." — **MATTHEW** 5:33-37

A promise is a promise. What difference does it make if you make your promise inside or outside a house of worship? A promise is a promise. God is present, watching and holding you to account regardless.
— **MATTHEW** 23:20-22

If those who get what God gives them only get it by doing everything they are told to do and filling out all the right forms properly signed, that eliminates personal trust completely and turns the promise into an ironclad *contract*! That's not a holy promise; that's a business deal. A contract drawn up by a hard-nosed lawyer and with plenty of fine print only makes sure that you will never be able to collect. But if there is no contract in the first place, simply a *promise* — and God's promise at that — you can't break it.

This is why the fulfillment of God's promise depends entirely on trusting God and his way, and then simply embracing him and what he does. God's promise arrives as pure gift. That's the only way everyone can be sure to get in on it, those who keep the religious traditions and those who have never heard of them. — ROMANS 4:14-16

Whatever God has promised gets stamped with the Yes of Jesus.
— 2 CORINTHIANS 1:20

My aim is to raise hopes by pointing the way to life without end. This is the life God promised long ago—and he doesn't break promises!
— TITUS 1:2

Let's keep a firm grip on the promises that keep us going. [God] always keeps his word. — HEBREWS 10:23

PURPOSE

We humans keep brainstorming options and plans,
        but GOD's purpose prevails. — PROVERBS 19:21

Form your purpose by asking for counsel,
        then carry it out using all the help you can get.
—PROVERBS 20:18

God's wisdom is something mysterious that goes deep into the interior of his purposes. You don't find it lying around on the surface. It's not the latest message, but more like the oldest — what God determined as the way to bring out his best in us, long before we ever arrived on the scene. — 1 CORINTHIANS 2:7

It's in Christ that we find out who we are and what we are living for. Long before we first heard of Christ and got our hopes up, he had his eye on us, had designs on us for glorious living, part of the overall purpose he is working out in everything and everyone. — EPHESIANS 1:11-12

The lines of purpose in your lives never grow slack, tightly tied as they are to your future in heaven, kept taut by hope.

The Message is as true among you today as when you first heard it. It doesn't diminish or weaken over time. — COLOSSIANS 1:5

We look at this Son and see the God who cannot be seen. We look at this Son and see God's original purpose in everything created. For everything, absolutely everything, above and below, visible and invisible, rank after rank after rank of angels — everything got started in him and finds its purpose in him. — COLOSSIANS 1:15-16

REBELLION

As long as we lived that old way of life, doing whatever we felt we could get away with, sin was calling most of the shots as the old law code hemmed us in. And this made us all the more rebellious. In the end, all we had to show for it was miscarriages and stillbirths.

— ROMANS 7:5

Who in the world do you think you are to second-guess God? Do you for one moment suppose any of us knows enough to call God into question? Clay doesn't talk back to the fingers that mold it, saying, "Why did you shape me like this?" — ROMANS 9:20

You yourselves are a case study of what he does. At one time you all had your backs turned to God, thinking rebellious thoughts of him, giving him trouble every chance you got. But now, by giving himself completely at the Cross, actually *dying* for you, Christ brought you over to God's side and put your lives together, whole and holy in his presence. You don't walk away from a gift like that!
— COLOSSIANS 1:21-23

Every part of Scripture is God-breathed and useful one way or another — showing us truth, exposing our rebellion, correcting our mistakes, training us to live God's way. — 2 TIMOTHY 3:16

[Jesus] offered himself as a sacrifice to free us from a dark, rebellious life into this good, pure life, making us a people he can be proud of, energetic in goodness. — TITUS 2:14

Since Jesus went through everything you're going through and more, learn to think like him. Think of your sufferings as a weaning from that old sinful habit of always expecting to get your own way. Then you'll be able to live out your days free to pursue what God wants instead of being tyrannized by what you want.

You've already put in your time in that God-ignorant way of life, partying night after night, a drunken and profligate life. Now it's time to be done with it for good. Of course, your old friends don't understand why you don't join in with the old gang anymore. But you don't have to give an account to them. They're the ones who will be called on the carpet — and before God himself. — 1 PETER 4:1-5

All who indulge in a sinful life are dangerously lawless, for sin is a major disruption of God's order. — 1 JOHN 3:4

RELATIONSHIPS

"Here is a simple, rule-of-thumb guide for behavior: Ask yourself what you want people to do for you, then grab the initiative and do it for them. Add up God's Law and Prophets and this is what you get."
— MATTHEW 7:12

"Don't pick on people, jump on their failures, criticize their faults — unless, of course, you want the same treatment. Don't condemn those who are down; that hardness can boomerang. Be easy on people; you'll find life a lot easier. Give away your life; you'll find life given back, but not merely given back — given back with bonus and blessing. Giving, not getting, is the way. Generosity begets generosity." — LUKE 6:37-38

Then [Jesus] turned to the host. "The next time you put on a dinner, don't just invite your friends and family and rich neighbors, the kind of people who will return the favor. Invite some people who never get invited out, the misfits from the wrong side of the tracks. You'll be — and experience — a blessing. They won't be able to return the favor, but the favor will be returned — oh, how it will be returned! — at the resurrection of God's people." — LUKE 14:12-14

Love from the center of who you are; don't fake it. Run for dear life from evil; hold on for dear life to good. Be good friends who love deeply; practice playing second fiddle.

Don't burn out; keep yourselves fueled and aflame. Be alert servants of the Master, cheerfully expectant. Don't quit in hard times; pray all the harder. Help needy Christians; be inventive in hospitality.

Bless your enemies; no cursing under your breath. Laugh with your happy friends when they're happy; share tears when they're down. Get along with each other; don't be stuck-up. Make friends with nobodies; don't be the great somebody.

Don't hit back; discover beauty in everyone. If you've got it in you, get along with everybody. — ROMANS 12:9-18

Don't run up debts, except for the huge debt of love you owe each other. When you love others, you complete what the law has been after all along. — ROMANS 13:8

Cultivate your own relationship with God, but don't impose it on others. You're fortunate if your behavior and your belief are coherent. — ROMANS 14:22

We don't evaluate people by what they have or how they look. We looked at the Messiah that way once and got it all wrong, as you know. We certainly don't look at him that way anymore. Now we look inside, and what we see is that anyone united with the Messiah gets a fresh start, is created new. The old life is gone; a new life burgeons! Look at it! All this comes from the God who settled the relationship between us and him, and then called us to settle our relationships with each other. — 2 CORINTHIANS 5:16-18

Live creatively, friends. If someone falls into sin, forgivingly restore him, saving your critical comments for yourself. You might be needing forgiveness before the day's out. Stoop down and reach out to those who are oppressed. Share their burdens, and so complete Christ's law. If you think you are too good for that, you are badly deceived.

Make a careful exploration of who you are and the work you have been given, and then sink yourself into that. Don't be impressed with yourself. Don't compare yourself with others. Each of you must take responsibility for doing the creative best you can with your own life. — GALATIANS 6:1-5

If you've gotten anything at all out of following Christ, if his love has made any difference in your life, if being in a community of the Spirit means anything to you, if you have a heart, if you care—then do me a favor: Agree with each other, love each other, be deep-spirited friends. Don't push your way to the front; don't sweet-talk your way to the top. Put yourself aside, and help others get ahead. Don't be obsessed with getting your own advantage. Forget yourselves long enough to lend a helping hand. — PHILIPPIANS 2:1-4

Be gracious in your speech. The goal is to bring out the best in others in a conversation, not put them down, not cut them out.
— COLOSSIANS 4:6

God's gift has restored our relationship with him and given us back our lives. And there's more life to come — an eternity of life!
— TITUS 3:7

Regard prisoners as if you were in prison with them. Look on victims of abuse as if what happened to them had happened to you.
— HEBREWS 13:3

Dear friend, when you extend hospitality to Christian brothers and sisters, even when they are strangers, you make the faith visible.
— 3 JOHN 5

REPUTATION

Earn a reputation for living well
    in God's eyes and the eyes of the people. — PROVERBS 3:4

A sterling reputation is better than striking it rich;
    a gracious spirit is better than money in the bank.
— PROVERBS 22:1

Don't call attention to yourself;
  let others do that for you. — **PROVERBS** 27:2

[Jesus said,] "Don't be naive. Some people will impugn your motives, others will smear your reputation — just because you believe in me." — **MATTHEW** 10:17

We don't want anyone suspecting us of taking one penny of this money for ourselves. We're being as careful in our reputation with the public as in our reputation with God. That's why we're sending another trusted friend along. He's proved his dependability many times over, and carries on as energetically as the day he started. — **2 CORINTHIANS** 8:20-22

As for those who were considered important in the church, their reputation doesn't concern me. God isn't impressed with mere appearances, and neither am I. — **GALATIANS** 2:6

Do you want to be counted wise, to build a reputation for wisdom? Here's what you do: Live well, live wisely, live humbly. It's the way you live, not the way you talk, that counts. — **JAMES** 3:13

RESPONSIBILITY

"Great gifts mean great responsibilities; greater gifts, greater responsibilities!" — **LUKE** 12:48

Those of us who are strong and able in the faith need to step in and lend a hand to those who falter, and not just do what is most convenient for us. Strength is for service, not status. — ROMANS 15:1

I'm not responsible for what the outsiders do, but don't we have some responsibility for those within our community of believers?
— 1 CORINTHIANS 5:12

If you choose to speak, you're also responsible for how and when you speak. — 1 CORINTHIANS 14:32

Each of you must take responsibility for doing the creative best you can with your own life. — GALATIANS 6:5

Anyone who neglects to care for family members in need repudiates the faith. That's worse than refusing to believe in the first place.
— 1 TIMOTHY 5:8

Our people have to learn to be diligent in their work so that all necessities are met (especially among the needy) and they don't end up with nothing to show for their lives. — TITUS 3:14

If you know the right thing to do and don't do it, that, for you, is evil.
— JAMES 4:17

REST

[Jesus said,] "Here's what I want you to do: Find a quiet, secluded place so you won't be tempted to role-play before God. Just be there as simply and honestly as you can manage. The focus will shift from you to God, and you will begin to sense his grace." — **MATTHEW** 6:6

"Are you tired? Worn out? Burned out on religion? Come to me. Get away with me and you'll recover your life. I'll show you how to take a real rest." — **MATTHEW** 11:28

Jesus said, "Come off by yourselves; let's take a break and get a little rest." For there was constant coming and going. They didn't even have time to eat.

So they got in the boat and went off to a remote place by themselves. — **MARK** 6:31-32

I want you woven into a tapestry of love, in touch with everything there is to know of God. Then you will have minds confident and at rest, focused on Christ, God's great mystery. — **COLOSSIANS** 2:2

SATISFACTION

God — you're my God!
I can't get enough of you! — **PSALM** 63:1

Well-spoken words bring satisfaction;
     well-done work has its own reward. — PROVERBS 12:14

Humans are satisfied with whatever looks good;
     GOD probes for what *is* good. — PROVERBS 16:2

Words satisfy the mind as much as fruit does the stomach;
     good talk is as gratifying as a good harvest. — PROVERBS 18:20

You're addicted to thrills? What an empty life!
     The pursuit of pleasure is never satisfied. — PROVERBS 21:17

"It's trouble ahead if you're satisfied with yourself.
     Your *self* will not satisfy you for long.
And it's trouble ahead if you think life's all fun and games.
     There's suffering to be met, and you're going to meet it."
— LUKE 6:25

I'm just as happy with little as with much, with much as with little. I've found the recipe for being happy whether full or hungry, hands full or hands empty. Whatever I have, wherever I am, I can make it through anything in the One who makes me who I am.
— PHILIPPIANS 4:12-13

Watch out for the Esau syndrome: trading away God's lifelong gift in order to satisfy a short-term appetite. — HEBREWS 12:16

SEEKING GOD

When my heart whispered, "Seek God,"
 my whole being replied,
"I'm seeking him!" — PSALM 27:8

Open up before GOD, keep nothing back;
 he'll do whatever needs to be done. — PSALM 37:5

Trust GOD from the bottom of your heart;
 don't try to figure out everything on your own.
Listen for GOD's voice in everything you do, everywhere you go;
 he's the one who will keep you on track.
Don't assume that you know it all.
 Run to GOD! Run from evil! — PROVERBS 3:5-7

The skeptic swore, "There is no God!
 No God!—I can do anything I want!" — PROVERBS 30:1

"Don't bargain with God. Be direct. Ask for what you need. This isn't a cat-and-mouse, hide-and-seek game we're in." — MATTHEW 7:7-8

"Don't look for shortcuts to God. The market is flooded with surefire, easygoing formulas for a successful life that can be practiced in your spare time. Don't fall for that stuff, even though crowds of people do."
— MATTHEW 7:13

[Jesus said,] "If your first concern is to look after yourself, you'll never find yourself. But if you forget about yourself and look to me, you'll find both yourself and me." — MATTHEW 10:39

"Self-help is no help at all. Self-sacrifice is the way, my way, to finding yourself, your true self. What kind of deal is it to get everything you want but lose yourself? What could you ever trade your soul for?"
— MATTHEW 16:25-26

"Anyone who examines this evidence will come to stake his life on this: that God himself is the truth." — JOHN 3:33

"It's who you are and the way you live that count before God. Your worship must engage your spirit in the pursuit of truth. That's the kind of people the Father is out looking for: those who are simply and honestly *themselves* before him in their worship. God is sheer being itself— Spirit. Those who worship him must do it out of their very being, their spirits, their true selves, in adoration." — JOHN 4:23-24

[Jesus said,] "You have your heads in your Bibles constantly because you think you'll find eternal life there. But you miss the forest for the trees. These Scriptures are all about *me*! And here I am, standing right before you, and you aren't willing to receive from me the life you say you want." — JOHN 5:39-40

"Don't be nitpickers; use your head — and heart! — to discern what is right, to test what is authentically right." — JOHN 7:24

"Then you will experience for yourselves the truth, and the truth will free you." — JOHN 8:32

Jesus then said, "I came into the world to bring everything into the clear light of day, making all the distinctions clear, so that those who have never seen will see, and those who have made a great pretense of seeing will be exposed as blind." — JOHN 9:39

Jesus said, "I am the Road, also the Truth, also the Life. No one gets to the Father apart from me." — JOHN 14:6

"The God who made the world and everything in it, this Master of sky and land, doesn't live in custom-made shrines or need the human race to run errands for him, as if he couldn't take care of himself. He makes the creatures; the creatures don't make him. Starting from scratch, he made the entire human race and made the earth hospitable, with plenty of time and space for living so we could seek after God, and not just grope around in the dark but actually *find* him. He doesn't play hide-and-seek with us. He's not remote; he's *near*. We live and move in him, can't get away from him! One of your poets said it well: 'We're the God-created.' Well, if we are the God-created, it doesn't make a lot of sense to think we could hire a sculptor to chisel a god out of stone for *us*, does it?

"God overlooks it as long as you don't know any better — but that time is past. The unknown is now known, and he's calling for a radical life-change. He has set a day when the entire human race will be judged and everything set right. And he has already appointed the judge, confirming him before everyone by raising him from the dead."
— ACTS 17:24-31

People try to put a shroud over truth. But the basic reality of God is plain enough. Open your eyes and there it is! By taking a long and thoughtful look at what God has created, people have always been able to see what their eyes as such can't see: eternal power, for instance, and the mystery of his divine being. So nobody has a good excuse. What happened was this: People knew God perfectly well, but when they didn't treat him like God, refusing to worship him, they trivialized themselves into silliness and confusion so that there was neither sense nor direction left in their lives. They pretended to know it all, but were illiterate regarding life. — ROMANS 1:18-22

[God said,] "Careful! I've put a huge stone on the road to Mount Zion,
    a stone you can't get around.
But the stone is me! If you're looking for me,
    you'll find me on the way, not in the way." — ROMANS 9:33

But how can people call for help if they don't know who to trust? And how can they know who to trust if they haven't heard of the One who can be trusted? And how can they hear if nobody tells them? And how is anyone going to tell them, unless someone is sent to do it?

— ROMANS 10:14-15

So where can you find someone truly wise, truly educated, truly intelligent in this day and age? Hasn't God exposed it all as pretentious nonsense? Since the world in all its fancy wisdom never had a clue when it came to knowing God, God in his wisdom took delight in using what the world considered dumb — *preaching*, of all things! — to bring those who trust him into the way of salvation.

While Jews clamor for miraculous demonstrations and Greeks go in for philosophical wisdom, we go right on proclaiming Christ, the Crucified. Jews treat this like an *anti*-miracle — and Greeks pass it off as absurd. But to us who are personally called by God himself — both Jews and Greeks — Christ is God's ultimate miracle and wisdom all wrapped up in one. Human wisdom is so tinny, so impotent, next to the seeming absurdity of God. Human strength can't begin to compete with God's "weakness." — 1 CORINTHIANS 1:20-25

We know only a portion of the truth, and what we say about God is always incomplete. But when the Complete arrives, our incompletes will be canceled. . . .

We don't yet see things clearly. We're squinting in a fog, peering through a mist. But it won't be long before the weather clears and the sun shines bright! We'll see it all then, see it all as clearly as God sees us, knowing him directly just as he knows us!

— 1 **CORINTHIANS** 13:9-10,12

It's impossible to please God apart from faith. And why? Because anyone who wants to approach God must believe both that he exists and that he cares enough to respond to those who seek him. — **HEBREWS** 11:6

Friends, this world is not your home, so don't make yourselves cozy in it. Don't indulge your ego at the expense of your soul. — 1 **PETER** 2:11

SELF-IMAGE

I look up at your macro-skies, dark and enormous,
    your handmade sky-jewelry,
Moon and stars mounted in their settings.
    Then I look at my micro-self and wonder,
Why do you bother with us?
    Why take a second look our way? — **PSALM** 8:3-4

"Live out your God-created identity. Live generously and graciously toward others, the way God lives toward you." — **MATTHEW** 5:48

[Jesus said,] "Self-help is no help at all. Self-sacrifice is the way, my way, to finding yourself, your true self. What good would it do to get everything you want and lose you, the real you?" — **LUKE** 9:24-25

"If you walk around with your nose in the air, you're going to end up flat on your face. But if you're content to be simply yourself, you will become more than yourself." — LUKE 14:11

Obsession with self . . . is a dead end; attention to God leads us out into the open, into a spacious, free life. Focusing on the self is the opposite of focusing on God. Anyone completely absorbed in self ignores God, ends up thinking more about self than God. That person ignores who God is and what he is doing. And God isn't pleased at being ignored. — ROMANS 8:6-8

Don't become so well-adjusted to your culture that you fit into it without even thinking. Instead, fix your attention on God. You'll be changed from the inside out. Readily recognize what he wants from you, and quickly respond to it. Unlike the culture around you, always dragging you down to its level of immaturity, God brings the best out of you, develops well-formed maturity in you. . . .

The only accurate way to understand ourselves is by what God is and by what he does for us, not by what we are and what we do for him. — ROMANS 12:2-3

Let's just go ahead and be what we were made to be, without enviously or pridefully comparing ourselves with each other, or trying to be something we aren't. — ROMANS 12:6

Don't you see that you can't live however you please, squandering what God paid such a high price for? The physical part of you is not some piece of property belonging to the spiritual part of you. God owns the whole works. — 1 CORINTHIANS 6:19-20

Now we look inside, and what we see is that anyone united with the Messiah gets a fresh start, is created new. The old life is gone; a new life burgeons! Look at it! — 2 CORINTHIANS 5:17

What you say about yourself means nothing in God's work. It's what God says about you that makes the difference.
— 2 CORINTHIANS 10:18

I have been crucified with Christ. My ego is no longer central. It is no longer important that I appear righteous before you or have your good opinion, and I am no longer driven to impress God. Christ lives in me. The life you see me living is not "mine," but it is lived by faith in the Son of God, who loved me and gave himself for me. — GALATIANS 2:20

Make a careful exploration of who you are and the work you have been given, and then sink yourself into that. Don't be impressed with yourself. Don't compare yourself with others. Each of you must take responsibility for doing the creative best you can with your own life.
— GALATIANS 6:4-5

It's in Christ that we find out who we are and what we are living for. Long before we first heard of Christ and got our hopes up, he had his eye on us, had designs on us for glorious living, part of the overall purpose he is working out in everything and everyone. — **EPHESIANS** 1:11-12

Whatever I have, wherever I am, I can make it through anything in the One who makes me who I am. — **PHILIPPIANS** 4:13

Don't fool yourself into thinking that you are a listener when you are anything but, letting the Word go in one ear and out the other. Act on what you hear! Those who hear and don't act are like those who glance in the mirror, walk away, and two minutes later have no idea who they are, what they look like. — **JAMES** 1:22-24

What matters is not your outer appearance — the styling of your hair, the jewelry you wear, the cut of your clothes — but your inner disposition.

Cultivate inner beauty, the gentle, gracious kind that God delights in. — 1 **PETER** 3:3-4

Be content with who you are, and don't put on airs. God's strong hand is on you; he'll promote you at the right time. Live carefree before God; he is most careful with you. — 1 **PETER** 5:6-7

SELFISHNESS

The world of the generous gets larger and larger;
the world of the stingy gets smaller and smaller.
— **PROVERBS** 11:24

[Jesus said,] "Self-help is no help at all. Self-sacrifice is the way, my way, to finding yourself, your true self. What kind of deal is it to get everything you want but lose yourself? What could you ever trade your soul for?" — MATTHEW 16:25-26

"Protect yourself against the least bit of greed. Life is not defined by what you have, even when you have a lot." — LUKE 12:15

Live freely, animated and motivated by God's Spirit. Then you won't feed the compulsions of selfishness. For there is a root of sinful self-interest in us that is at odds with a free spirit, just as the free spirit is incompatible with selfishness. — GALATIANS 5:16-17

It is obvious what kind of life develops out of trying to get your own way all the time: repetitive, loveless, cheap sex; a stinking accumulation of mental and emotional garbage; frenzied and joyless grabs for happiness; trinket gods; magic-show religion; paranoid loneliness; cutthroat competition; all-consuming-yet-never-satisfied wants; a brutal temper; an impotence to love or be loved; divided homes and divided lives; small-minded and lopsided pursuits; the vicious habit of depersonalizing everyone into a rival; uncontrolled and uncontrollable addictions; ugly parodies of community. I could go on. . . .

If you use your freedom this way, you will not inherit God's kingdom. — GALATIANS 5:19-21

Don't push your way to the front; don't sweet-talk your way to the top. Put yourself aside, and help others get ahead. Don't be obsessed with getting your own advantage. Forget yourselves long enough to lend a helping hand. — PHILIPPIANS 2:3-4

Let the peace of Christ keep you in tune with each other, in step with each other. None of this going off and doing your own thing.
— COLOSSIANS 3:15

You're cheating on God. If all you want is your own way, flirting with the world every chance you get, you end up enemies of God and his way. — JAMES 4:4

Since Jesus went through everything you're going through and more, learn to think like him. Think of your sufferings as a weaning from that old sinful habit of always expecting to get your own way. Then you'll be able to live out your days free to pursue what God wants instead of being tyrannized by what you want. — 1 PETER 4:1-2

Don't love the world's ways. Don't love the world's goods. Love of the world squeezes out love for the Father. Practically everything that goes on in the world — wanting your own way, wanting everything for yourself, wanting to appear important — has nothing to do with the Father. It just isolates you from him. The world and all its wanting, wanting, wanting is on the way out — but whoever does what God wants is set for eternity. — 1 JOHN 2:15-17

This is how we've come to understand and experience love: Christ sacrificed his life for us. This is why we ought to live sacrificially for our fellow believers, and not just be out for ourselves. If you see some brother or sister in need and have the means to do something about it but turn a cold shoulder and do nothing, what happens to God's love? It disappears. And you made it disappear. — 1 JOHN 3:16-17

SENSITIVITY

Compassion doesn't originate in our bleeding hearts or moral sweat, but in God's mercy. — ROMANS 9:16

Isn't it wonderful all the ways in which this distress has goaded you closer to God? You're more alive, more concerned, more sensitive, more reverent, more human, more passionate, more responsible. Looked at from any angle, you've come out of this with purity of heart.
— 2 CORINTHIANS 7:11

Be gentle with one another, sensitive. Forgive one another as quickly and thoroughly as God in Christ forgave you. — EPHESIANS 4:32

Be energetic in your life of salvation, reverent and sensitive before God. That energy is God's energy, an energy deep within you, God himself willing and working at what will give him the most pleasure.
— PHILIPPIANS 2:12-13

Gently encourage the stragglers, and reach out for the exhausted, pulling them to their feet. Be patient with each person, attentive to individual needs. — 1 THESSALONIANS 5:14

Be agreeable, be sympathetic, be loving, be compassionate, be humble. — 1 PETER 3:8

Don't lose a minute in building on what you've been given, complementing your basic faith with good character, spiritual understanding, alert discipline, passionate patience, reverent wonder, warm friendliness, and generous love, each dimension fitting into and developing the others. — 2 PETER 1:5-7

SEX

Bless your fresh-flowing fountain!
    Enjoy the wife you married as a young man!
Lovely as an angel, beautiful as a rose —
    don't ever quit taking delight in her body.
Never take her love for granted! — PROVERBS 5:18-19

There's more to sex than mere skin on skin. Sex is as much spiritual mystery as physical fact. As written in Scripture, "The two become one." Since we want to become spiritually one with the Master, we must not pursue the kind of sex that avoids commitment and intimacy, leaving us more lonely than ever — the kind of sex that can never

"become one." There is a sense in which sexual sins are different from all others. In sexual sin we violate the sacredness of our own bodies, these bodies that were made for God-given and God-modeled love, for "becoming one" with another. Or didn't you realize that your body is a sacred place, the place of the Holy Spirit? Don't you see that you can't live however you please, squandering what God paid such a high price for? The physical part of you is not some piece of property belonging to the spiritual part of you. God owns the whole works. So let people see God in and through your body.
— 1 CORINTHIANS 6:16-20

Is it a good thing to have sexual relations?

Certainly — but only within a certain context. It's good for a man to have a wife, and for a woman to have a husband. Sexual drives are strong, but marriage is strong enough to contain them and provide for a balanced and fulfilling sexual life in a world of sexual disorder. The marriage bed must be a place of mutuality — the husband seeking to satisfy his wife, the wife seeking to satisfy her husband. Marriage is not a place to "stand up for your rights." Marriage is a decision to serve the other, whether in bed or out. Abstaining from sex is permissible for a period of time if you both agree to it, and if it's for the purposes of prayer and fasting — but only for such times. Then come back together again. Satan has an ingenious way of tempting us when we least expect it. — 1 CORINTHIANS 7:1-5

No test or temptation that comes your way is beyond the course of what others have had to face. All you need to remember is that God

will never let you down; he'll never let you be pushed past your limit; he'll always be there to help you come through it.
— 1 CORINTHIANS 10:13

Don't allow love to turn into lust, setting off a downhill slide into sexual promiscuity, filthy practices, or bullying greed. Though some tongues just love the taste of gossip, Christians have better uses for language than that. Don't talk dirty or silly. That kind of talk doesn't fit our style. Thanksgiving is our dialect. — EPHESIANS 5:3-4

A man leaves father and mother and cherishes his wife. No longer two, they become "one flesh." — EPHESIANS 5:31

God wants you to live a pure life.

Keep yourselves from sexual promiscuity.

Learn to appreciate and give dignity to your body, not abusing it, as is so common among those who know nothing of God.
— 1 THESSALONIANS 4:3-5

Honor marriage, and guard the sacredness of sexual intimacy between wife and husband. God draws a firm line against casual and illicit sex.
— HEBREWS 13:4

The one who blesses others is abundantly blessed;
    those who help others are helped. — **PROVERBS** 11:25

Mercy to the needy is a loan to GOD,
    and GOD pays back those loans in full. — **PROVERBS** 19:17

"When you do something for someone else, don't call attention to yourself. You've seen them in action, I'm sure — 'playactors' I call them — treating prayer meeting and street corner alike as a stage, acting compassionate as long as someone is watching, playing to the crowds. They get applause, true, but that's all they get. When you help someone out, don't think about how it looks. Just do it — quietly and unobtrusively. That is the way your God, who conceived you in love, working behind the scenes, helps you out." — **MATTHEW** 6:2-4

"Here is a simple, rule-of-thumb guide for behavior: Ask yourself what you want people to do for you, then grab the initiative and do it for them." — **MATTHEW** 7:12

"You have been treated generously, so live generously."
— **MATTHEW** 10:8

"If you only give for what you hope to get out of it, do you think that's charity? The stingiest of pawnbrokers does that. . . .

"Give away your life; you'll find life given back, but not merely given back — given back with bonus and blessing. Giving, not getting, is the way. Generosity begets generosity." — LUKE 6:34,38

Then [Jesus] turned to the host. "The next time you put on a dinner, don't just invite your friends and family and rich neighbors, the kind of people who will return the favor. Invite some people who never get invited out, the misfits from the wrong side of the tracks. You'll be — and experience — a blessing. They won't be able to return the favor, but the favor will be returned — oh, how it will be returned! — at the resurrection of God's people." — LUKE 14:12-14

They committed themselves to the teaching of the apostles, the life together, the common meal, and the prayers.

Everyone around was in awe — all those wonders and signs done through the apostles! And all the believers lived in a wonderful harmony, holding everything in common. They sold whatever they owned and pooled their resources so that each person's need was met.

They followed a daily discipline of worship in the Temple followed by meals at home, every meal a celebration, exuberant and joyful.
— ACTS 2:42-46

The whole congregation of believers was united as one — one heart, one mind! They didn't even claim ownership of their own possessions. No one said, "That's mine; you can't have it." They shared everything.
— ACTS 4:32

Help needy Christians; be inventive in hospitality. — **ROMANS** 12:13

I want each of you to take plenty of time to think it over, and make up your own mind what you will give. That will protect you against sob stories and arm-twisting. God loves it when the giver delights in the giving.

God can pour on the blessings in astonishing ways so that you're ready for anything and everything, more than just ready to do what needs to be done. — 2 **CORINTHIANS** 9:7-8

Stoop down and reach out to those who are oppressed. Share their burdens, and so complete Christ's law. If you think you are too good for that, you are badly deceived. — **GALATIANS** 6:2-3

Be very sure now, you who have been trained to a self-sufficient maturity, that you enter into a generous common life with those who have trained you, sharing all the good things that you have and experience.
— **GALATIANS** 6:6

Make sure you don't take things for granted and go slack in working for the common good; share what you have with others. God takes particular pleasure in acts of worship — a different kind of "sacrifice" — that take place in kitchen and workplace and on the streets.
— **HEBREWS** 13:16

SINGLENESS

Better to live alone in a tumbledown shack
than share a mansion with a nagging spouse. — **PROVERBS** 21:9

Sometimes I wish everyone were single like me — a simpler life in many ways! But celibacy is not for everyone any more than marriage is. God gives the gift of the single life to some, the gift of the married life to others.

I do, though, tell the unmarried and widows that singleness might well be the best thing for them, as it has been for me.
— 1 **CORINTHIANS** 7:7-8

If a wife should leave her husband, she must either remain single or else come back and make things right with him. And a husband has no right to get rid of his wife. — 1 **CORINTHIANS** 7:11

I want you to live as free of complications as possible. When you're unmarried, you're free to concentrate on simply pleasing the Master. Marriage involves you in all the nuts and bolts of domestic life and in wanting to please your spouse, leading to so many more demands on your attention. The time and energy that married people spend on caring for and nurturing each other, the unmarried can spend in becoming whole and holy instruments of God. I'm trying to be help-ful and make it as easy as possible for you, not make things harder. All I want is for you to be able to develop a way of life in which you can spend plenty of time together with the Master without a lot of distractions. — 1 **CORINTHIANS** 7:32-35

Be brave. Be strong. Don't give up.
>Expect GOD to get here soon. — **PSALM** 31:24

Less is more and more is less.
>One righteous will outclass fifty wicked,
For the wicked are moral weaklings
>but the righteous are GOD-strong. — **PSALM** 37:16-17

Invigorate my soul so I can praise you well,
>use your decrees to put iron in my soul. — **PSALM** 119:175

Our Lord is great, with limitless strength;
>we'll never comprehend what he knows and does.
— **PSALM** 147:5

It's better to be wise than strong;
>intelligence outranks muscle any day. — **PROVERBS** 24:5

Those of us who are strong and able in the faith need to step in and lend a hand to those who falter, and not just do what is most convenient for us. Strength is for service, not status. — **ROMANS** 15:1

Human wisdom is so tinny, so impotent, next to the seeming absurdity of God. Human strength can't begin to compete with God's "weakness."
— 1 CORINTHIANS 1:25

We felt like we'd been sent to death row, that it was all over for us. As it turned out, it was the best thing that could have happened. Instead of trusting in our own strength or wits to get out of it, we were forced to trust God totally — not a bad idea since he's the God who raises the dead! — 2 CORINTHIANS 1:9

I quit focusing on the handicap and began appreciating the gift. It was a case of Christ's strength moving in on my weakness. Now I take limitations in stride, and with good cheer, these limitations that cut me down to size — abuse, accidents, opposition, bad breaks. I just let Christ take over! And so the weaker I get, the stronger I become.
— 2 CORINTHIANS 12:9-10

Are you going to continue this craziness? For only crazy people would think they could complete by their own efforts what was begun by God. If you weren't smart enough or strong enough to begin it, how do you suppose you could perfect it? — GALATIANS 3:3

We pray that you'll live well for the Master, making him proud of you as you work hard in his orchard. As you learn more and more how God works, you will learn how to do your work. We pray that you'll have the strength to stick it out over the long haul — not the grim strength of gritting your teeth but the glory-strength God gives. It is strength that endures the unendurable and spills over into joy, thanking the Father who makes us strong enough to take part in everything bright and beautiful that he has for us. — COLOSSIANS 1:10-12

STRESS

Pile your troubles on GOD's shoulders —
    he'll carry your load, he'll help you out. — PSALM 55:22

[God,] you've kept track of my every toss and turn
    through the sleepless nights,
Each tear entered in your ledger,
    each ache written in your book. — PSALM 56:8

I'm awake all night — not a wink of sleep;
    I can't even say what's bothering me.
I go over the days one by one,
    I ponder the years gone by. — PSALM 77:4-5

The minute I said, "I'm slipping, I'm falling,"
    your love, GOD, took hold and held me fast.
When I was upset and beside myself,
    you calmed me down and cheered me up. — PSALM 94:18-19

People who won't settle down, wandering hither and yon,
are like restless birds flitting to and fro. — **PROVERBS** 27:8

"If you decide for God, living a life of God-worship, it follows that you don't fuss about what's on the table at mealtimes or whether the clothes in your closet are in fashion. There is far more to your life than the food you put in your stomach, more to your outer appearance than the clothes you hang on your body. . . .

"What I'm trying to do here is to get you to relax, to not be so preoccupied with *getting*, so you can respond to God's giving. People who don't know God and the way he works fuss over these things, but you know both God and how he works. Steep your life in God-reality, God-initiative, God-provisions. Don't worry about missing out. You'll find all your everyday human concerns will be met.

"Give your entire attention to what God is doing right now, and don't get worked up about what may or may not happen tomorrow. God will help you deal with whatever hard things come up when the time comes." — **MATTHEW** 6:25,31-34

[Jesus said,] "Are you tired? Worn out? Burned out on religion? Come to me. Get away with me and you'll recover your life. I'll show you how to take a real rest. Walk with me and work with me — watch how I do it. Learn the unforced rhythms of grace. I won't lay anything heavy or ill-fitting on you. Keep company with me and you'll learn to live freely and lightly." — **MATTHEW** 11:28-30

Don't fret or worry. Instead of worrying, pray. Let petitions and praises shape your worries into prayers, letting God know your concerns.

PROMISES. PROMISES. PROMISES.

Before you know it, a sense of God's wholeness, everything coming together for good, will come and settle you down. It's wonderful what happens when Christ displaces worry at the center of your life.

— **PHILIPPIANS** 4:6-7

SUCCESS

Refuse good advice and watch your plans fail;
take good counsel and watch them succeed. — **PROVERBS** 15:22

"Don't look for shortcuts to God. The market is flooded with surefire, easygoing formulas for a successful life that can be practiced in your spare time. Don't fall for that stuff, even though crowds of people do. The way to life — to God! — is vigorous and requires total attention."

— **MATTHEW** 7:13-14

"Whoever wants to be great must become a servant."

— **MATTHEW** 20:26

"It's not possible for a person to succeed — I'm talking about eternal success — without heaven's help." — **JOHN** 3:27

I pray for good fortune in everything you do, and for your good health — that your everyday affairs prosper, as well as your soul!

— 3 **JOHN** 2

SUFFERING

My troubles turned out all for the best —
> they forced me to learn from [GOD's] textbook.

— **PSALM** 119:71

"You're blessed when your commitment to God provokes persecution. The persecution drives you even deeper into God's kingdom."

— **MATTHEW** 5:10

Walking down the street, Jesus saw a man blind from birth. His disciples asked, "Rabbi, who sinned: this man or his parents, causing him to be born blind?"

Jesus said, "You're asking the wrong question. You're looking for someone to blame. There is no such cause-effect here. Look instead for what God can do." — **JOHN** 9:1-3

"I'm leaving you well and whole. That's my parting gift to you. Peace. I don't leave you the way you're used to being left — feeling abandoned, bereft. So don't be upset." — **JOHN** 14:27

"Anyone signing up for the kingdom of God has to go through plenty of hard times." — **ACTS** 14:22

We continue to shout our praise even when we're hemmed in with troubles, because we know how troubles can develop passionate patience in us, and how that patience in turn forges the tempered steel of virtue, keeping us alert for whatever God will do next.

— **ROMANS** 5:3-4

All around us we observe a pregnant creation. The difficult times of pain throughout the world are simply birth pangs. But it's not only around us; it's *within* us. The Spirit of God is arousing us within. We're also feeling the birth pangs. These sterile and barren bodies of ours are yearning for full deliverance. That is why waiting does not diminish us, any more than waiting diminishes a pregnant mother. We are enlarged in the waiting. — **ROMANS** 8:22-24

Better to be confronted by the Master now than to face a fiery confrontation later. — 1 **CORINTHIANS** 11:32

Distress that drives us to God does that. It turns us around. It gets us back in the way of salvation. We never regret that kind of pain. But those who let distress drive them away from God are full of regrets, end up on a deathbed of regrets. — 2 **CORINTHIANS** 7:10

Because of the extravagance of those revelations, and so I wouldn't get a big head, I was given the gift of a handicap to keep me in constant touch with my limitations. Satan's angel did his best to get me down; what he in fact did was push me to my knees. No danger then of walking around high and mighty! At first I didn't think of it as a gift, and begged God to remove it. Three times I did that, and then he told me,

My grace is enough; it's all you need.
My strength comes into its own in your weakness.

Once I heard that, I was glad to let it happen. I quit focusing on the handicap and began appreciating the gift. It was a case of Christ's strength moving in on my weakness. Now I take limitations in stride, and with good cheer, these limitations that cut me down to size — abuse, accidents, opposition, bad breaks. I just let Christ take over! And so the weaker I get, the stronger I become.
— 2 CORINTHIANS 12:7-10

There's far more to this life than trusting in Christ. There's also suffering for him. And the suffering is as much a gift as the trusting.
— PHILIPPIANS 1:29

I didn't want some petty, inferior brand of righteousness that comes from keeping a list of rules when I could get the robust kind that comes from trusting Christ — God's righteousness.
I gave up all that inferior stuff so I could know Christ personally, experience his resurrection power, be a partner in his suffering, and go all the way with him to death itself. — PHILIPPIANS 3:9-10

It was a beautiful thing that you came alongside me in my troubles.
— PHILIPPIANS 4:14

Anyone who wants to live all out for Christ is in for a lot of trouble; there's no getting around it. — 2 TIMOTHY 3:12

While he lived on earth, anticipating death, Jesus cried out in pain and wept in sorrow as he offered up priestly prayers to God. Because he honored God, God answered him. Though he was God's Son, he learned trusting-obedience by what he suffered, just as we do.
— **HEBREWS** 5:7-8

Consider it a sheer gift, friends, when tests and challenges come at you from all sides. You know that under pressure, your faith-life is forced into the open and shows its true colors. So don't try to get out of anything prematurely. Let it do its work so you become mature and well-developed, not deficient in any way. — **JAMES** 1:2-4

Pure gold put in the fire comes out of it proved pure; genuine faith put through this suffering comes out proved genuine. — **1 PETER** 1:7

There's no particular virtue in accepting punishment that you well deserve. But if you're treated badly for good behavior and continue in spite of it to be a good servant, that is what counts with God.

This is the kind of life you've been invited into, the kind of life Christ lived. He suffered everything that came his way so you would know that it could be done, and also know how to do it, step-by-step.
— **1 PETER** 2:20-21

Since Jesus went through everything you're going through and more, learn to think like him. Think of your sufferings as a weaning from that old sinful habit of always expecting to get your own way. Then you'll be able to live out your days free to pursue what God wants instead of being tyrannized by what you want. — 1 PETER 4:1-2

Keep your guard up. You're not the only ones plunged into these hard times. It's the same with Christians all over the world. So keep a firm grip on the faith. The suffering won't last forever. — 1 PETER 5:9-10

TEMPTATION

If bad companions tempt you,
    don't go along with them. — PROVERBS 1:10

"Stay alert; be in prayer so you don't wander into temptation without even knowing you're in danger. There is a part of you that is eager, ready for anything in God. But there's another part that's as lazy as an old dog sleeping by the fire." — MATTHEW 26:41

Don't be so naive and self-confident. You're not exempt. You could fall flat on your face as easily as anyone else. Forget about self-confidence; it's useless. Cultivate God-confidence.

No test or temptation that comes your way is beyond the course of what others have had to face. All you need to remember is that God will never let you down; he'll never let you be pushed past your limit; he'll always be there to help you come through it.

— 1 CORINTHIANS 10:12-13

Take everything the Master has set out for you, well-made weapons of the best materials. And put them to use so you will be able to stand up to everything the Devil throws your way. This is no afternoon athletic contest that we'll walk away from and forget about in a couple of hours. This is for keeps, a life-or-death fight to the finish against the Devil and all his angels.

Be prepared. You're up against far more than you can handle on your own. Take all the help you can get, every weapon God has issued, so that when it's all over but the shouting you'll still be on your feet. Truth, righteousness, peace, faith, and salvation are more than words. Learn how to apply them. You'll need them throughout your life.
— EPHESIANS 6:11-17

Now that we know what we have — Jesus, this great High Priest with ready access to God — let's not let it slip through our fingers. We don't have a priest who is out of touch with our reality. He's been through weakness and testing, experienced it all — all but the sin. So let's walk right up to him and get what he is so ready to give. Take the mercy, accept the help. — HEBREWS 4:14-16

Consider it a sheer gift, friends, when tests and challenges come at you from all sides. You know that under pressure, your faith-life is forced into the open and shows its true colors. — JAMES 1:2-3

Anyone who meets a testing challenge head-on and manages to stick it out is mighty fortunate. For such persons loyally in love with God, the reward is life and more life.

Don't let anyone under pressure to give in to evil say, "God is trying to trip me up." God is impervious to evil, and puts evil in no one's way. The temptation to give in to evil comes from us and only us. We have no one to blame but the leering, seducing flare-up of our own lust. Lust gets pregnant, and has a baby: sin! Sin grows up to adulthood, and becomes a real killer. — JAMES 1:12-15

I know how great this makes you feel, even though you have to put up with every kind of aggravation in the meantime. Pure gold put in the fire comes out of it *proved* pure; genuine faith put through this suffering comes out *proved* genuine. When Jesus wraps this all up, it's your faith, not your gold, that God will have on display as evidence of his victory. — 1 PETER 1:6-7

TIREDNESS

A cheerful disposition is good for your health;
    gloom and doom leave you bone-tired. — PROVERBS 17:22

[Jesus said,] "Are you tired? Worn out? Burned out on religion? Come to me. Get away with me and you'll recover your life. I'll show you how to take a real rest. Walk with me and work with me — watch how I do it. Learn the unforced rhythms of grace. I won't lay anything heavy or ill-fitting on you. Keep company with me and you'll learn to live freely and lightly." — MATTHEW 11:28-30

Don't burn out; keep yourselves fueled and aflame. Be alert servants of the Master. — **ROMANS** 12:11

Let's not allow ourselves to get fatigued doing good. At the right time we will harvest a good crop if we don't give up, or quit. — **GALATIANS** 6:9

TRUST

I hate all this silly religion,
    but you, GOD, I trust. — **PSALM** 31:6

Blessed are you who give yourselves over to GOD,
    turn your backs on the world's "sure thing,"
    ignore what the world worships. — **PSALM** 40:4

Trust [God] absolutely, people;
    lay your lives on the line for him. — **PSALM** 62:8

Far better to take refuge in GOD
    than trust in people;
Far better to take refuge in GOD
    than trust in celebrities. — **PSALM** 118:8-9

Trust GOD from the bottom of your heart;
    don't try to figure out everything on your own.

Listen for GOD's voice in everything you do, everywhere you go;
    he's the one who will keep you on track. — PROVERBS 3:5-6

A gadabout gossip can't be trusted with a secret,
    but someone of integrity won't violate a confidence.
— PROVERBS 11:13

It pays to take life seriously;
    things work out when you trust in GOD. — PROVERBS 16:20

Those who think they can do it on their own end up obsessed with measuring their own moral muscle but never get around to exercising it in real life. Those who trust God's action in them find that God's Spirit is in them — living and breathing God! — ROMANS 8:5

How can people call for help if they don't know who to trust? And how can they know who to trust if they haven't heard of the One who can be trusted? And how can they hear if nobody tells them? And how is anyone going to tell them, unless someone is sent to do it?
— ROMANS 10:14-15

God, who got you started in this spiritual adventure, shares with us the life of his Son and our Master Jesus. He will never give up on you. Never forget that. — 1 CORINTHIANS 1:9

Now God has us where he wants us, with all the time in this world and the next to shower grace and kindness upon us in Christ Jesus. Saving is all his idea, and all his work. All we do is trust him enough to let him do it. It's God's gift from start to finish! — EPHESIANS 2:7-8

When we trust in him, we're free to say whatever needs to be said, bold to go wherever we need to go. — EPHESIANS 3:12

The One who called you is completely dependable. If he said it, he'll do it! — 1 THESSALONIANS 5:24

If we give up on [God], he does not give up — for there's no way he can be false to himself. — 2 TIMOTHY 2:13

TRUTH

What you're after is truth from the inside out.
    Enter me, then; conceive a new, true life. — PSALM 51:6

The more talk, the less truth;
    the wise measure their words. — PROVERBS 10:19

Truth lasts;
    lies are here today, gone tomorrow. — PROVERBS 12:19

Humans are satisfied with whatever looks good;
>   GOD probes for what *is* good. — PROVERBS 16:2

"There's trouble ahead when you live only for the approval of others, saying what flatters them, doing what indulges them. Popularity contests are not truth contests — look how many scoundrel preachers were approved by your ancestors! Your task is to be true, not popular." — LUKE 6:26

Anyone who examines this evidence will come to stake his life on this: that God himself is the truth. — JOHN 3:33

"It's who you are and the way you live that count before God. Your worship must engage your spirit in the pursuit of truth. That's the kind of people the Father is out looking for: those who are simply and honestly themselves before him in their worship." — JOHN 4:23

"Don't be nitpickers; use your head — and heart! — to discern what is right, to test what is authentically right." — JOHN 7:24

[Jesus said,] "If you stick with this, living out what I tell you, you are my disciples for sure. Then you will experience for yourselves the truth, and the truth will free you." — JOHN 8:31-32

We know only a portion of the truth, and what we say about God is always incomplete. — 1 CORINTHIANS 13:9

We refuse to wear masks and play games. We don't maneuver and manipulate behind the scenes. And we don't twist God's Word to suit ourselves. Rather, we keep everything we do and say out in the open, the whole truth on display, so that those who want to can see and judge for themselves in the presence of God.
— 2 CORINTHIANS 4:2

We use our powerful God-tools for smashing warped philosophies, tearing down barriers erected against the truth of God, fitting every loose thought and emotion and impulse into the structure of life shaped by Christ. — 2 CORINTHIANS 10:5

Concentrate on doing your best for God, work you won't be ashamed of, laying out the truth plain and simple. — 2 TIMOTHY 2:15

Every part of Scripture is God-breathed and useful one way or another—showing us truth, exposing our rebellion, correcting our mistakes, training us to live God's way. — 2 TIMOTHY 3:16

Use the truth to either spur people on in knowledge or stop them in their tracks if they oppose it. — TITUS 1:9

Twisting the truth to make yourselves sound wise isn't wisdom.
— JAMES 3:14

My dear friends, if you know people who have wandered off from God's truth, don't write them off. Go after them. Get them back.
— JAMES 5:19

UNDERSTANDING

It takes wisdom to build a house,
    and understanding to set it on a firm foundation.
— PROVERBS 24:3

Like the horizons for breadth and the ocean for depth,
    the understanding of a good leader is broad and deep.
— PROVERBS 25:3

When the country is in chaos,
    everybody has a plan to fix it —
But it takes a leader of real understanding
    to straighten things out. — PROVERBS 28:2

"Your ears are open but you don't hear a thing.
Your eyes are awake but you don't see a thing." — MATTHEW 13:14

The only accurate way to understand ourselves is by what God is and by what he does for us, not by what we are and what we do for him.
— ROMANS 12:3

Knowing isn't everything. If it becomes everything, some people end up as know-it-alls who treat others as know-nothings. Real knowledge isn't that insensitive. — 1 CORINTHIANS 8:7

Remember how you were when you didn't know God, led from one phony god to another, never knowing what you were doing, just doing it because everybody else did it? It's different in this life. God wants us to use our intelligence, to seek to understand as well as we can.
— 1 CORINTHIANS 12:2

Love never dies. Inspired speech will be over some day; praying in tongues will end; understanding will reach its limit. We know only a portion of the truth, and what we say about God is always incomplete. But when the Complete arrives, our incompletes will be canceled.
— 1 CORINTHIANS 13:8-10

We don't yet see things clearly. We're squinting in a fog, peering through a mist. But it won't be long before the weather clears and the sun shines bright! We'll see it all then, see it all as clearly as God sees us, knowing him directly just as he knows us! — 1 CORINTHIANS 13:12

Summing it all up, friends, I'd say you'll do best by filling your minds and meditating on things true, noble, reputable, authentic, compelling, gracious — the best, not the worst; the beautiful, not the ugly; things to praise, not things to curse. — **PHILIPPIANS** 4:8

Be assured that from the first day we heard of you, we haven't stopped praying for you, asking God to give you wise minds and spirits attuned to his will, and so acquire a thorough understanding of the ways in which God works. — **COLOSSIANS** 1:9

VIOLENCE

Violence boomerangs. — **PSALM** 7:16

Evil people are restless
    unless they're making trouble;
They can't get a good night's sleep
    unless they've made life miserable for somebody.
Perversity is their food and drink,
    violence their drug of choice. — **PROVERBS** 4:16-17

"Here's another old saying that deserves a second look: 'Eye for eye, tooth for tooth.' Is that going to get us anywhere? Here's what I propose: 'Don't hit back at all.' If someone strikes you, stand there and take it. If someone drags you into court and sues for the shirt off your back, giftwrap your best coat and make a present of it. And if someone takes unfair advantage of you, use the occasion to practice the servant life. No more tit-for-tat stuff. Live generously." — MATTHEW 5:38-42

Bless your enemies; no cursing under your breath. Laugh with your happy friends when they're happy; share tears when they're down. Get along with each other; don't be stuck-up. Make friends with nobodies; don't be the great somebody.

Don't hit back; discover beauty in everyone. If you've got it in you, get along with everybody. Don't insist on getting even; that's not for you to do. "I'll do the judging," says God. "I'll take care of it." . . .

Don't let evil get the best of you; get the best of evil by doing good. — ROMANS 12:14-19,21

Where do you think all these appalling wars and quarrels come from? Do you think they just happen? Think again. They come about because you want your own way, and fight for it deep inside yourselves. You lust for what you don't have and are willing to kill to get it. You want what isn't yours and will risk violence to get your hands on it.

You wouldn't think of just asking God for it, would you? And why not? Because you know you'd be asking for what you have no right to. You're spoiled children, each wanting your own way.
— JAMES 4:1-3

WEAKNESS

God-devotion makes a country strong;
    God-avoidance leaves people weak. — PROVERBS 14:34

[Jesus said,] "I am the Vine, you are the branches. When you're joined with me and I with you, the relation intimate and organic, the harvest is sure to be abundant. Separated, you can't produce a thing."
— JOHN 15:5

Welcome with open arms fellow believers who don't see things the way you do. And don't jump all over them every time they do or say something you don't agree with — even when it seems that they are strong on opinions but weak in the faith department. Remember, they have their own history to deal with. Treat them gently. — ROMANS 14:1

Human wisdom is so tinny, so impotent, next to the seeming absurdity of God. Human strength can't begin to compete with God's "weakness."
— 1 CORINTHIANS 1:25

If I have to "brag" about myself, I'll brag about the humiliations that make me like Jesus. — 2 CORINTHIANS 11:30

And then [God] told me,

> My grace is enough; it's all you need.
> My strength comes into its own in your weakness.

Once I heard that, I was glad to let it happen. I quit focusing on the handicap and began appreciating the gift. It was a case of Christ's strength moving in on my weakness. Now I take limitations in stride,

and with good cheer, these limitations that cut me down to size —
abuse, accidents, opposition, bad breaks. I just let Christ take over!
And so the weaker I get, the stronger I become.
— 2 CORINTHIANS 12:9-10

WISDOM

[God,] with your very own hands you formed me;
now breathe your wisdom over me so I can understand you.
— PSALM 119:73

Become wise by walking with the wise;
hang out with fools and watch your life fall to pieces.
— PROVERBS 13:20

Foolish dreamers live in a world of illusion;
wise realists plant their feet on the ground. — PROVERBS 14:18

Get wisdom — it's worth more than money;
choose insight over income every time. — PROVERBS 16:16

Wise men and women are always learning,
always listening for fresh insights. — PROVERBS 18:15

Knowing what is right is like deep water in the heart;
a wise person draws from the well within. — PROVERBS 20:5

It's better to be wise than strong;

   intelligence outranks muscle any day. — **PROVERBS** 24:5

A wise friend's timely reprimand

   is like a gold ring slipped on your finger. — **PROVERBS** 25:12

If you think you know it all, you're a fool for sure;

   real survivors learn wisdom from others. — **PROVERBS** 28:26

Human wisdom is so tinny, so impotent, next to the seeming absurdity of God. Human strength can't begin to compete with God's "weakness." — **1 CORINTHIANS** 1:25

Don't fool yourself. Don't think that you can be wise merely by being up-to-date with the times. — **1 CORINTHIANS** 3:18

We never really know enough until we recognize that God alone knows it all. — **1 CORINTHIANS** 8:3

Do you want to be counted wise, to build a reputation for wisdom? Here's what you do: Live well, live wisely, live humbly. It's the way you live, not the way you talk, that counts. Mean-spirited ambition isn't wisdom. Boasting that you are wise isn't wisdom. Twisting the truth to make yourselves sound wise isn't wisdom. It's the furthest thing from wisdom — it's animal cunning, devilish conniving. Whenever you're trying to look better than others or get the better of others, things fall apart and everyone ends up at the others' throats.

Real wisdom, God's wisdom, begins with a holy life and is characterized by getting along with others. It is gentle and reasonable, overflowing with mercy and blessings, not hot one day and cold the next, not two-faced. — JAMES 3:13-17

WORK

Well-done work has its own reward. — PROVERBS 12:14

The diligent find freedom in their work;
    the lazy are oppressed by work. — PROVERBS 12:24

GOD cares about honesty in the workplace;
    your business is his business. — PROVERBS 16:11

Appetite is an incentive to work;
    hunger makes you work all the harder. — PROVERBS 16:26

Observe people who are good at their work — skilled workers are always in demand and admired. — PROVERBS 22:29

"You don't need a lot of equipment. You are the equipment, and all you need to keep that going is three meals a day. Travel light."
— MATTHEW 10:10

Don't burn out; keep yourselves fueled and aflame. Be alert servants of the Master. — ROMANS 12:11

Don't hold back. Throw yourselves into the work of the Master, confident that nothing you do for him is a waste of time or effort.
— 1 CORINTHIANS 15:58

We have no intention of moving in on what others have done and taking credit for it. "If you want to claim credit, claim it for God." What you say about yourself means nothing in God's work. It's what God says about you that makes the difference.
— 2 CORINTHIANS 10:16-18

Get an honest job so that you can help others who can't work.
— EPHESIANS 4:28

As long as I'm alive in this body, there is good work for me to do.
— PHILIPPIANS 1:22

We pray that you'll live well for the Master, making him proud of you as you work hard in his orchard. As you learn more and more how God works, you will learn how to do your work. We pray that you'll have the strength to stick it out over the long haul — not the grim strength of gritting your teeth but the glory-strength God gives. It is strength that endures the unendurable. — COLOSSIANS 1:10-11

Servants, do what you're told by your earthly masters. And don't just do the minimum that will get you by. Do your best. Work from the heart for your real Master, for God, confident that you'll get paid in full when you come into your inheritance. Keep in mind always that the ultimate Master you're serving is Christ. — COLOSSIANS 3:22-24

And masters, treat your servants considerately. Be fair with them. Don't forget for a minute that you, too, serve a Master — God in heaven. — COLOSSIANS 4:1

Stay calm; mind your own business; do your own job. You've heard all this from us before, but a reminder never hurts. We want you living in a way that will command the respect of outsiders, not lying around sponging off your friends. — 1 THESSALONIANS 4:11-12

Get along among yourselves, each of you doing your part. Our counsel is that you warn the freeloaders to get a move on. Gently encourage the stragglers, and reach out for the exhausted, pulling them to their feet. Be patient with each person, attentive to individual needs. — 1 THESSALONIANS 5:13-14

Our orders — backed up by the Master, Jesus — are to refuse to have anything to do with those among you who are lazy and refuse to work the way we taught you. Don't permit them to freeload on the rest. . . .

Don't you remember the rule we had when we lived with you? "If you don't work, you don't eat." And now we're getting reports that a bunch of lazy good-for-nothings are taking advantage of you. This must not be tolerated. We command them to get to work immediately — no excuses, no arguments — and earn their own keep. Friends, don't slack off in doing your duty. — 2 THESSALONIANS 3:6,10-13

WORRY

Worry weighs us down;
    a cheerful word picks us up. — PROVERBS 12:25

Don't fret or worry. Instead of worrying, pray. Let petitions and praises shape your worries into prayers, letting God know your concerns. Before you know it, a sense of God's wholeness, everything coming together for good, will come and settle you down. It's wonderful what happens when Christ displaces worry at the center of your life.
— PHILIPPIANS 4:6-7

If you don't know what you're doing, pray to the Father. He loves to help. You'll get his help, and won't be condescended to when you ask for it. Ask boldly, believingly, without a second thought. People who "worry their prayers" are like wind-whipped waves. Don't think you're going to get anything from the Master that way, adrift at sea, keeping all your options open. — JAMES 1:5-8

Let's not just talk about love; let's practice real love. This is the only way we'll know we're living truly, living in God's reality. It's also the way to shut down debilitating self-criticism, even when there is something to it. For God is greater than our worried hearts and knows more about us than we do ourselves. — 1 JOHN 3:18-20